# THE

# ARSENAL SHIP

## ACQUISITION PROCESS EXPERIENCE

Contrasting and Common Impressions from the
Contractor Teams and Joint Program Office

| ROBERT S. LEONARD | JEFFREY A. DREZNER | GEOFFREY SOMMER |

Prepared for the
DEFENSE ADVANCED RESEARCH PROJECTS AGENCY

NATIONAL DEFENSE RESEARCH INSTITUTE

## RAND

The research described in this report was sponsored by the Defense Advanced Research Projects Agency. The research was conducted in RAND's National Defense Research Institute, a federally funded research and development center supported by the Office of the Secretary of Defense, the Joint Staff, the unified commands, and the defense agencies under Contract DASW01-95-C-0059.

**Library of Congress Cataloging-in-Publication Data**

Leonard, Robert S.
  The arsenal ship acquisition process experience : contrasting and
common impressions from the contractor teams and joint program office /
Robert S. Leonard, Jeffrey A. Drezner, Geoffrey Sommer.
     p.    cm.
  "Prepared for the Defense Advanced Research Projects Agency
(DARPA) by RAND's National Defense Research Institute."
  "MR-1030-DARPA."
  Includes bibliographical references (p. ).
  ISBN 0-8330-2690-9
  1. United States. Navy—Procurement.  2. United States. Navy—
Weapons systems—Costs.  3. Warships—United States—Design and
construction.  4. Shipbuilding—United States.  I. Drezner, Jeffrey A.
II. Sommer, Geoffrey, 1957– .  III. United States. Defense Advanced
Research Projects Agency.  IV. National Defense Research Institute
(U.S.).  V. Title.
VC263.L42   1999
359.6 ' 212 ' 0973—dc21                                          98-52862
                                                                      CIP

RAND is a nonprofit institution that helps improve policy and decisionmaking through research and analysis. RAND® is a registered trademark. RAND's publications do not necessarily reflect the opinions or policies of its research sponsors.

Published 1999 by RAND
1700 Main Street, P.O. Box 2138, Santa Monica, CA 90407-2138
1333 H St., N.W., Washington, D.C. 20005-4707
RAND URL: http://www.rand.org/
To order RAND documents or to obtain additional information,
contact Distribution Services: Telephone: (310) 451-7002;
Fax: (310) 451-6915; Internet: order@rand.org

Assimilating the experiences of acquisition programs is an important element of process improvement. What is learned from programs using nontraditional acquisition strategies is especially important. One such program was the Arsenal Ship, a joint DARPA/ Navy program managed by DARPA (Defense Advanced Research Projects Agency). The objective of this research is to understand the Arsenal Ship program management experience and to distill lessons from it in order to improve the management of similar innovative acquisition programs, and to disseminate those lessons to the broader acquisition community. This report should interest DoD officials concerned with weapon system acquisition processes.

This study covers the duration of the Arsenal Ship program, from March 1996 through December 1997. The plans for the entire program, the events of the first two acquisition phases, and the circumstances leading to the program's cancellation near the end of Phase II are documented.

This research was sponsored by the Arsenal Ship Joint Program Office in DARPA. It was conducted by the Acquisition and Technology Policy Center of RAND's National Defense Research Institute, a federally funded research and development center sponsored by the Office of the Secretary of Defense, the Joint Staff, and the defense agencies.

# CONTENTS

Appendix

# FIGURES

# TABLES

# SUMMARY

## BACKGROUND

The Arsenal Ship acquisition program was unique in two respects: it represented a new operational concept for Navy ships, and its management structure and process were different from traditional military ship-building programs. The Arsenal Ship program was, in effect, an experiment in both product and process.

Three specific goals of the program were outlined at its inception: demonstrate the capability affordably; leverage commercial practices and technologies; and, demonstrate the reformed acquisition process. This research focuses on the program's acquisition strategy.

Our study of the Arsenal Ship program has several related purposes:

- To describe both the planned acquisition process and what actually transpired

- To define the program's outcomes in terms of what was expected, what occurred, and how these outcomes compare to a traditional acquisition approach

- To identify advantageous facets of the approach that might be adopted by current and future acquisition efforts.

## Program Structure

The Arsenal Ship program plan had six phases. Phase I spanned just six months, with cost-performance tradeoff studies leading to an initial design concept as its focus. Phase II involved developing the proposed concept into a functional design over a 12-month period. Phase III, had it occurred, was to have focused on the detailed design and construction of the Arsenal Ship Demonstrator,[1] and the detailed design of the production Arsenal Ship, over a 33-month time span. Phase IV was to be a one-year test and evaluation focusing on demonstrating the Arsenal Ship's military utility and determining how well it satisfies the Ship Capabilities Document (SCD) and Concept of Operations (CONOPS). Phase V involved a production option of five ships and a conversion option of the demonstrator to the production configuration. Phase VI was a "to be determined" option for service life-cycle support tasks for the fleet of six Arsenal Ships.

The program completed Phases I and II before ending in cancellation after just 20 months. The program was established 18 March 1996. Six teams competed for Phase I work. In July 1996, each of the five winning contractor teams was awarded $1 million Agreements.[2] Phase II Agreements of $15 million each were awarded to three contractor teams in January 1997, though the original plan called for a down-select to only two contractor teams. The inclusion of a third design team was a result of the desire to continue involvement of expertise and technologies unique to that team, providing additional options to the ASJPO for a relatively small additional investment in R & D dollars.[3]

The program was officially canceled 24 October 1997. The contractor teams submitted their Functional Designs three weeks later, com-

---

[1]This ship was subsequently renamed the Maritime Fire Support Demonstrator (MFSD) as a result of the April 1997 reorientation of the Arsenal Ship program to support the Navy's proposed 21st Century Surface Combatant program (SC 21). We will use the term "demonstrator" to refer to both designations throughout this report.

[2]An Agreement is an alternative to traditional contracts. See Chapter Three.

[3]The additional $15 million R&D funding is not small, based on the Arsenal Ship budget for FY97, but is small in the context of the planned production program or the overall DoD R&D budget.

pleting their Phase II payable milestones.  Phase III proposals were not submitted.  The official reason given for the program's termination was insufficient funding for FY98.

## Acquisition Approach

The acquisition approach for the Arsenal Ship was a major departure from traditional Navy ship programs, and from acquisition programs in general.  Key attributes of the acquisition strategy and process included:

* the use of a relatively few broad performance goals in describing desired system capabilities

* giving full design responsibility to the competing contractor teams, and facilitating this via excluding Government Furnished Equipment (GFE) from the program

* using a small joint program office

* designating affordability as the only requirement, and putting an emphasis on a small crew size

* structuring the program around DARPA's Section 845 Other Transactions Authority (OTA).

Utilizing the Section 845 OTA to structure and execute the program provided the flexibility to build the program around having the contractors demonstrate the *operational* performance of the weapon system instead of demonstrating *engineering* performance through detailed specifications.  The absence of detailed requirements and system specifications, coupled with the transfer of design responsibility from the government to the contractor teams, was the most striking aspect of the acquisition approach.  The flexibility provided by the absence of detailed hard requirements and the flow-down of those requirements to subcontractors provided the opportunity to create unique system concepts through design tradeoffs within a vastly larger solution space than a traditional approach affords.  The approach gave the contractors a feeling of empowerment and facilitated what both sides described as "common sense acquisition."

The transferring of design responsibility from the government to the contractors required cultural changes.  The contractors had to develop their own system specifications and make cost-performance trade decisions for themselves. The program office had to back away from providing direction to the contractors regarding their proposed systems' capabilities, and the design solutions providing those capabilities.

The small joint program office facilitated the acquisition process. The small size of the ASJPO succeeded through a hand-picked, highly qualified, and ideologically motivated staff, and through leveraged knowledge of selected external government experts who were "borrowed" at key junctures. The ASJPO's purpose was not typical of joint program offices. The joint DARPA/Navy office was formed to leverage DARPA's knowledge and experience with the OTA acquisition construct.[4]

The affordability emphasis manifested itself throughout the planned life cycle of the program. Development funding was fixed at the program's inception. Production costs, which were also established at the program's inception, were specified in the form of a Unit Sailaway Price (USP) goal and a not-to-exceed USP threshold. Operating and support costs were to be minimized primarily through use of a small crew. The fixed development funding proved to be inadequate; this adversely affected the contractors' belief that they would be able to meet the USP goal as well as demonstrate the small crew size. They still believed, however, that the USP threshold was achievable. The inadequate development funding forced deferral of nonrecurring efforts to the production portion of the program. The small crew size was seen as achievable on production Arsenal Ships, but not on the demonstrator due to the insufficient nonrecurring developmental funding.

## Issues Related to the Acquisition Strategy

Circumstances and events that related to the program's acquisition approach directly caused difficulties within the program for the ASJPO, the contractors, or both. External influences created an environment in which some issues were not addressed, even with aware-

---

[4]Joint program offices typically are formed to ensure that the weapon system meets the requirements of the multiple services for which it is being procured.

ness that these issues would not go away, and in some cases would only get worse. A discussion of some of the more important unresolved issues follows.

The contractor teams believed that the most serious problem was the underfunding of Phase III. The underfunding was the result of a combination of factors. Analysis prior to program initiation for estimation of the required developmental resources was inadequate. A miscommunication at the beginning of the program regarding resources perceived to be required greatly contributed to the underfunding. Finally, the magnitude of development tasks required to make the concept a reality was poorly understood and therefore underestimated.

Interactions with the Naval Surface Warfare Center (NSWC) labs and Navy PARticipating Managers (PARMs) were problematic. Because this was not a Navy program, neither the ASJPO nor contractor teams had the authority to compel these traditional acquisition-community organizations to provide information and access to data or equipment. Neither the labs nor PARMs had incentives to cooperate with the program. If the program had continued, both the contractors and ASJPO expected that relations with the PARMs in particular would have worsened.

Throughout the 20 months of the program's life, the ASJPO steadfastly adhered to the "program of record"; that is, the plan as envisioned at its inception. Early on, the contractors noted that changes in the program's acquisition approach toward a more traditional one would make the program all but impossible to execute within the schedule and funding. By the middle of Phase II, the contractors encouraged the ASJPO to abandon the program of record in light of the Navy senior leadership's program reorientation toward a demonstrator in support of both the Arsenal Ship and SC 21 programs, and away from production Arsenal Ships.

The contractor teams felt that providing an irrevocable USP offer at the end of Phase II was impractical. The immaturity of the design fostered their belief that the offered USP would not survive to production in Phase V. Some teams believed that, if the irrevocable offer did survive, its coupling with the fixed development funding and the technical matrix in the Phase III proposal amounted to fixed price development. The ASJPO disagreed regarding both the practicality of the irrevocable offer and the charge of fixed price development.

The notion of converting the demonstrator to the production configuration became problematic by the end of Phase II. The contractors cited insufficient Phase-III funding, the absence of a conversion price goal, and use of the ship to support the SC 21 program as deterrents. The vessel's modification to support the SC 21 program was not defined; thus, its state when returned to the contractor for conversion was not predictable. The ASJPO stated that, as a result, the conversion option probably could not be exercised contractually. These circumstances led the contractors to disregard the cost of the demonstrator's conversion, and believe that they would never be required to perform it. Their proposed designs reflected this.

## Why the Program Ended

The course of the program was determined by weak Navy support and by gross underfunding of Phase III. Had the Navy supported the program, the funding might have been corrected.

One might describe the results of the acquisition approach as cruelly ironic. The freedom it afforded within the program provided for great success *internally* in achieving goals applicable to its first two phases. However, the approach also created uncertainty and even hostility in the *external* forces relevant to it, namely stakeholders in the greater Navy community and those with agendas in Congress. These forces caused the program's cancellation.

The authors are not alone in our belief that the Navy's tepid support for this program was the determining factor in its cancellation. DARPA specifically stated that the program was canceled as a result of a lack of funding in fiscal year 1998, which was a direct result of "the Navy's poorly articulated and ambiguous legislative strategy for the Demonstrator."[5] We assert that, had the Navy truly wanted the program, its legislative strategy would have been clear.

---

[5]DARPA's 30 October 1997 letter to the program's three contractor teams in which the Phase III solicitation was canceled.

In the first two program phases, the competitive environment pressured the contractors into an unrealistic "can-do" attitude toward developing the Arsenal Ship within the planned funding. The open and honest relationship that the acquisition approach afforded between the contractors and ASJPO was not enough to counteract this pressure. The ASJPO was unable to resolve the insufficient-funding issue, even though they knew the program required additional funds to field an adequate demonstrator. The inability to increase program funding was a result of the ASJPO's commitment to staying within the originally specified $520 million budget, as well as the lack of support for the program in Congress and from key Naval community stakeholders.

The execution of the acquisition approach deteriorated as Phase II transpired due to the program's external environment. The contractors became less and less committed as a result of the erosion of support for the program within Congress, the Navy reorienting the program toward the SC/DD 21 and away from production Arsenal Ships in April 1997, and the program office's apparent inability to change the program in reaction to these factors.

## CONCLUSIONS AND IMPLICATIONS

The cancellation of the Arsenal Ship program precluded the ability to determine comprehensively the success or failure of its acquisition approach. Regarding the three specific goals of the program as outlined at its inception:

- It *did not* sufficiently mature to demonstrate the capability affordably.

- It *did* mature to the point where one can conclude that it leveraged commercial practices and technologies.

- It *partially* demonstrated the reformed acquisition process; that is, it did so for pre-detailed design and development activities in a competitive environment.

The program's development-phase funding and schedule proved to be problematic. The combined length of Phases I and II was too short, in the opinion of the program office and most of the contractor teams. The Phase III schedule appeared workable, providing contractor reliance on potentially uncooperative Navy organizations such as PARMs produced no pitfalls. The contractors were expected to (and did) buy into the first two phases, each spending about $5 million in Phase I and matching the government's $15 million in Phase II.

Overall impressions of the program structure and acquisition approach were generally positive at the end of Phase I. Most of the key attributes of the acquisition strategy were providing the results the program office wanted. By the middle of Phase II, the contractors had fully adjusted to the acquisition approach and liked it. The ASJPO described the contractor teams' work as outstanding. In discussions after the program had been officially cancelled, both program office and contractor personnel expressed disappointment in having to return to the inefficient, bureaucratic, constrained, and confrontational business practices of their traditional acquisition environments.

An innovative acquisition strategy similar to that used in the Arsenal Ship program should be implemented as a package. While the key elements of the strategy are distinct and identifiable, they interact with each other in a complex fashion. The elements of the acquisition strategy—minimal weapon system specification, contractor design responsibility, small joint program office, affordability constraints, integrated product and process teams, Section 845 OTA—are mutually enabling and reinforcing when properly executed.

The acquisition approach was only tested in the program's early stages, and only in an environment in which competition between contractors still existed. We cannot overstate how different the relationship between the government and winning contractor team likely would have been once competition was removed. At that point, the sole contractor team could afford to be both more straightforward and less agreeable with the government.

## Residual Effects

The influence that the Arsenal Ship program's acquisition approach and technical innovations have already had and will continue to have—on the CVN77 and subsequent aircraft carriers, and the DD21 and other ships in the SC21 class—appears to be significant.

At the inception of the Arsenal Ship program, the Navy's RDT&E portfolio showed the system concept as a high priority. As a result, when the Navy backed away from the concept, it incorporated some Arsenal Ship concept and mission aspects into the SC/DD 21 program. The DD 21 now reflects a low-observable design emphasis and anticipates a crew size of 95. Streamlined acquisition using a Section 845/804 OTA approach is now mandated for the first two phases of the DD 21 program.[6] As of this writing, facets of the Arsenal Ship's acquisition process, and personnel key to that process's implementation, are being used in the development and integration of the island and topside for the next two new aircraft carriers.

In the end, DARPA and the Navy spent $64–71 million on the Arsenal Ship/Maritime Fire Support Demonstrator program. They left the ASJPO, as a component of the DD 21 program, substantially intact and funded through March 1998. In the five months after the Arsenal Ship program's cancellation, the program office's charter was to transfer lessons learned to the DD 21 program. As a direct result of the Arsenal Ship/MFSD program experience, the Navy should put to sea more innovative and less-expensive-to-operate twenty-first century aircraft carriers and destroyers. It should benefit from reduced costs in designing, developing, producing, and operating and maintaining these ships. These effects may save many times over the expenditures of the Arsenal Ship/MFSD program.

---

[6]DD 21 Phase I Program Solicitation (Agreement No: N00024-98-R-2300), Part 1— Program Description, Objectives and Solicitation Response Instructions, Section 3— Acquisition Approach, March 1998.

# ACKNOWLEDGMENTS

We are grateful to our sponsor, the Arsenal Ship Joint Program Office, for their support and the unprecedented access to their staff and documentation they provided. In particular, we are indebted to Cindy Shaver for her guidance and assistance in leveraging the wealth of information within the ASJPO. We are equally appreciative of the contractors involved in the Arsenal Ship program, whose candor and generous cooperation made this research interesting, insightful, and (we believe) truly useful to the acquisition policymaker.

We are also indebted to RAND colleagues Tim Bonds, Mark Lorell, and Giles Smith, who added considerably to the form and content of this work throughout its development. Their comments, plus the input of the contractor and consulting communities in the form of document reviews from Tomas Egan, Robert Johnson, Ron Kiss, Sam Marshall, John Treadway, and John Turner, made this document as comprehensive and accurate as possible. Any remaining errors of omission or commission are the sole responsibility of the authors.

| | |
|---|---|
| ACAT | Acquisition Category |
| ACTD | Advanced Concept Technology Demonstrator |
| AOA | Analysis of Alternatives |
| ASJPO | Arsenal Ship Joint Program Office |
| ASOS | Arsenal Ship Offboard Systems |
| ATWCS | Advanced Tomahawk Weapon Control System |
| BAFO | Best and Final Offer |
| $C^4I$ | Command, Control, Communications, Computers, and Intelligence |
| CAIV | Cost As an Independent Variable |
| CBO | Congressional Budget Office |
| CEC | Cooperative Engagement Capability |
| CICA | Competition In Contracting Act |
| CINC | Commander in Chief |
| COEA | Cost and Operational Effectiveness Analysis |
| CONOPS | Concept of Operations |
| CRS | Congressional Research Service |
| CVX | Next Generation Aircraft Carrier |
| DAB | Defense Acquisition Board |
| DARPA | Defense Advanced Research Projects Agency |
| DD 21 | 21st Century Land Attack Destroyer |
| DFAR | Defense Federal Acquisition Regulation |
| DoD | Department of Defense |
| DSB | Defense Science Board |

| | |
|---|---|
| FAR | Federal Acquisition Regulation |
| GAO | General Accounting Office |
| GDP | Gross Domestic Product |
| GFE | Government Furnished Equipment |
| HAE UAV | High Altitude Endurance Unmanned Aerial Vehicle |
| IMP | Integrated Master Plan |
| IMS | Integrated Master Schedule |
| IPPT | Integrated Product and Process Team |
| IPT | Integrated Product Team *or* Integrated Process Team |
| IR&D | Individual Research and Development |
| LCS | Launch Control System |
| LRIP | Low Rate Initial Production |
| MDAP | Major Defense Acquisition Program |
| MFSD | Maritime Fire Support Demonstrator |
| MNS | Mission Need Statement |
| MOA | Memorandum of Agreement |
| MRC | Major Regional Contingency |
| NAVSEA | Naval Sea Systems Command |
| NRAC | Naval Research Advisory Committee |
| NRE | Non-Recurring Engineering |
| NSWC | Naval Surface Warfare Center |
| ONR | Office of Naval Research |
| ORD | Operational Requirements Document |
| OTA | Other Transactions Authority |
| OTS | Off The Shelf |
| PARM | PARticipating Manager |
| POM | Program Objective Memorandum |
| R&D | Research and Development |
| RDT&E | Research, Development, Test, and Evaluation |
| RFP | Request For Proposal |
| SAR | Selected Acquisition Report |
| SC 21 | 21st Century Surface Combatant |
| SCD | Ship Capabilities Document |

| | |
|---|---|
| SRD | System Requirements Document |
| TDD | Task Description Document |
| TEMP | Technical Engineering Management Plan |
| TRA | Teledyne Ryan Aerospace |
| TRP | Technology Reinvestment Project |
| TSSE | Total Ship System Engineering |
| UFP | Unit Flyaway Price |
| USP | Unit Sailaway Price |
| VLS | Vertical Launch System |

# Chapter One

# INTRODUCTION

As part of a broad effort to improve the weapon system acquisition process, the Department of Defense (DoD) has undertaken several initiatives focused on demonstrating innovative and nontraditional approaches to acquisition. Advanced Concept Technology Demonstrators (ACTDs), which emphasize the rapid infusion of mature technology and new capability to the warfighter, are one example. The "Other Transactions Authority" (OTA) granted under Section 845 of the FY94 Defense Authorization Act,[1] which allows the Defense Advanced Research Project Agency (DARPA) and other DoD agencies and components to manage programs outside the traditional set of acquisition regulations, is another.[2]

Two ongoing acquisition efforts—the High Altitude Endurance Unmanned Air Vehicle (HAE UAV) programs, composed of the Global Hawk and DarkStar aircraft—are managed under the ACTD approach. The Global Hawk program began in mid-1994, and served the Arsenal Ship Joint Program Office (ASJPO) as the model for the Arsenal Ship's acquisition process.[3]

---

[1]Public Law 103-160, Section 845 (107 STAT. 1721). Other Transactions is authorized under 10 U.S.C. 2371.

[2]The original law included only DARPA. The law was revised in FY97 to include other DoD agencies and components.

[3]RAND is also studying these ACTD programs. Phase I of the Global Hawk HAE UAV program has been documented in RAND report MR-809-DARPA.

The ASJPO has documented the Arsenal Ship program from its per-spective.[4] Its document provides a much richer account of the technical achievements of the program and the day-to-day program-office affairs, but covers the acquisition strategy in less detail and does not capture the contractor teams' perspectives as do we. In the areas that the two documents overlap, they mostly concur. The ex-ception is that herein we withhold judgment regarding many of the program's aspects. We believe that, for many of them, a determina-tion of their success or failure would be premature.

## MOTIVATION BEHIND THE ARSENAL SHIP CONCEPT AND PROGRAM APPROACH

At the inception of the Arsenal Ship program, the system concept was characterized as a high priority in the Navy's Research, Development, Test, and Evaluation (RDT&E) portfolio.[5] The Navy intended the weapon system to buttress its recent shift in emphasis from open-ocean conflict to support of joint land and littoral warfighting capabilities in regional conflicts. The system was to "provide the theater commander with massive firepower, long range strike, and flexible targeting and possible theater defense through the availability of hundreds of VLS [Vertical Launch System] cells."[6] The Arsenal Ship concept was tailored specifically to be stationed continuously forward, and meet fire-support needs in the initial stages of conflict.

Unique critical technical attributes of the Arsenal Ship concept in-cluded an array of vertical missile launchers, off-board targeting, command, and control in a "remote missile magazine," minimal crew size (no more than 50), passive survivability, and flexible and robust data links and overall information architecture. The weapon

---

[4]*Arsenal Ship Lessons Learned,* 31 December 1997, by Charles S. Hamilton, Capt. USN, Arsenal Ship Program Manager.

[5]Joint Memorandum, Subj: ARSENAL SHIP PROGRAM, March 18, 1996; Memorandum of Agreement (MOA), Joint Navy/DARPA Arsenal Ship Demonstration Program, May 1996, signed by the Director, DARPA, the Assistant Secretary of the Navy for Research, Development, and Acquisition, and the Director, Surface Warfare Division.

[6]Joint Memorandum, Subj: ARSENAL SHIP PROGRAM, 18 March 1996. See Ap-pendix F.

system concept's capabilities included long-range strike, naval surface fire support, and theater air defense.

The Arsenal Ship program, a joint Navy/DARPA program managed
by a DARPA Joint Program Office, was conducted using a unique and
innovative acquisition approach employing the OTA.  The program
was not an ACTD.  The approach provided a significant opportunity
to streamline program management and use innovative business
management concepts.  The program's approach was intended to
facilitate:

- streamlined contracting methods

- early industry involvement in the development cycle, in order to
  get the Navy out of the ship-design business

- involvement of nontraditional suppliers

- development of a cooperative industry-government team with
  government "insight not oversight" approach to management

- multiple innovative design solutions derived using a Total Ship
  Systems Engineering (TSSE) approach that takes advantage of
  the best off-the-shelf commercial and military systems, as well as
  new development systems where optimal

- operator/user design input and system evaluation prior to production commitment

- lower overall system cost for development, production, and operating and support

- a shortened acquisition cycle.

## RESEARCH APPROACH AND OBJECTIVES

Our research approach required that we work closely with both the
ASJPO and contractor teams.  RAND's research team worked under
the same nondisclosure agreements as the ASJPO, and had complete
access to ASJPO files and personnel.  In addition to our informal
interactions with ASJPO officials, we conducted formal interviews
with the contractor teams and ASJPO members at the completion of
each program phase.  Our research objectives were to:

- Document the experience of the program.

- Compare the experience of the Arsenal Ship with traditional ship-acquisition programs.

- Understand the extent to which the nontraditional elements of the program's acquisition strategy affect program outcomes.

- Distill lessons from the Arsenal Ship program management experience.

- Determine which lessons from this experience can be beneficially leveraged for application in the broader acquisition community.

Our research effort spanned the life of the Arsenal Ship program. Our approach included:

- observing the acquisition strategies employed by the ASJPO, identifying the key elements of the strategy that define the Arsenal Ship's uniqueness, and tracking how those key elements were implemented

- collecting relevant information and documentation from the ASJPO and contractors, and observing ASJPO and contractor reactions through a series of focus interviews and discussions

- identifying and describing the relationships between the unique aspects of the acquisition strategy and program outcomes, determining how contractors exploited the opportunities inherent in the acquisition strategy, and how those innovative and nontraditional acquisition practices affected program outcomes (cost, schedule, performance, risk management, etc.).

## ORGANIZATION OF THIS REPORT

Chapter Two provides an overview of the intended program plan and actual events. It includes details on the program phases and their funding, the winning contractor teams in Phases I and II, and the specific down-select criteria for award in Phases II and III. Chapter Three discusses the Arsenal Ship program's acquisition strategy, key differences with traditional acquisition approaches, and rationale for the strategy. Chapter Four provides a brief overview of the traditional Navy ship acquisition process, and how the Arsenal Ship program differed.  Also included is a comparison of the program's schedule to that planned for the SC/DD 21 program through award of detailed design and lead-ship construction.

Chapter Five focuses on implementation of the program's unique process by presenting insights and opinions from interviews with the contractor teams and the ASJPO.  We report their experiences during Phases I and II.  Chapter Five explores differences of opinion and perception between contractor teams and the ASJPO.  Chapter Six, also drawn from the interviews, outlines issues that arose during Phases I and II.  We discuss how these issues were resolved, or were expected to affect future program phases.  Chapter Seven contains our analysis of the program.  We examine why the contractors continued with the program through its cancellation, the reasons behind the cancellation, and the successes and failures of the acquisition approach.  We then compare the program's experience to similar streamlined acquisition programs currently under study at RAND.

Appendix A provides a brief history of the genesis of the Arsenal Ship concept.  Appendix B identifies key technical characteristics of the Arsenal Ship program that make it unique among ship-acquisition programs.  Appendix C provides comparisons of the program's planned schedule and cost from award of detailed design and lead-ship/demonstrator-ship construction through delivery.  Appendix D contains the Ship Capabilities Document (SCD); Appendix E, the Concept of Operations (CONOPS); Appendix F, the Joint Memorandum establishing the program; and, Appendix G, the Joint Memorandum defining the Joint Navy/DARPA program.

# Chapter Two

# ARSENAL SHIP PROGRAM OVERVIEW

This chapter provides an overview of the planned program and actual execution experience. It is meant to provide context for understanding the contrasts between the Arsenal Ship's unique acquisition
approach and that of more traditional programs. Details of the program execution are discussed in subsequent chapters.

## PROGRAM DEFINITION

A simple two-page joint memorandum established the Arsenal Ship
Program as a non-Acquisition Category program and outlined the
general management approach and performance characteristics of
the system.[1]  DARPA was given program lead for its early phases to
take advantage of its Section 845 OTA, and to facilitate transfer of its
innovative business practices to the Navy acquisition community.
The program was expected to transition to Navy leadership at a later
phase.

A subsequent Memorandum of Agreement (MOA) between DARPA
and the Navy further defined the management approach.[2]  The MOA
specified two program goals: evaluate the new operational capability
embodied in the Arsenal Ship, and exploit DARPA's culture and experience in streamlined prototyping and technology development
programs to accelerate the Navy's ongoing acquisition-reform ef-

---

[1]Joint Memorandum, ARSENAL SHIP PROGRAM, March 18, 1996. See Appendix F.

[2]Memorandum of Agreement, Joint Navy/DARPA Arsenal Ship Demonstration
Program, May 1996. See Appendix G.

forts. The MOA also set up a Steering Committee and an Executive Committee for guidance and oversight.[3]

Through its involvement in this program, the Navy hoped to learn the "DARPA process," described as giving program responsibility to industry in a competitive environment. This process used the OTA in this instance, but is not viewed as necessarily associated with it in general. Senior members of Naval Sea Systems Command (NAVSEA) management are supportive of the Section 845 process; they intend to demonstrate the feasibility and advantages of this method in a future mainstream program managed within the Navy.

The Arsenal Ship program plan called for six phases. The schedule for the first four is shown in Figure 2.1. Throughout the 20-month life of the program, all milestones were met as planned.

## Phase I Solicitation and Description

The Phase I Solicitation was a "radical departure" from a traditional DoD Request for Proposal (RFP), in that "offerors are requested to propose their own unique program approach which will best satisfy the Department of Defense's objectives."[4] Each offeror was asked to propose an Agreement for evaluation, rather than the government specifying a contract to be negotiated.

The solicitation was written to provide the contractors with the government's "vision" for the complete program. The government explained the planned schedule and funding profile through the development and operational demonstration of the demonstrator ship, Phases I–IV. Detailed criteria were given for the down-select decision to Phase II.

---

[3]The Steering Committee includes the Director, TTO, DARPA, the Deputy Assistant Secretary of the Navy (Ships), Assistant Director, TTO, DARPA, the Director, Surface Warfare Plans/Programs/Requirements Branch, the PEO for Surface Combatants, and the Office of Naval Research. The Executive Committee includes the Director, DARPA, the Assistant Secretary of the Navy (RD&A), Director of Surface Warfare, Commander, NAVSEA, and the Chief of Naval Research.

[4]Arsenal Ship Program Solicitation (MDA972-96-R-0001), dated 23 May 1996.

RAND*MR1030-1*

| ID | Task Name | Start | Finish | FY96 Q (1\|2\|3\|4) | FY97 Q (1\|2\|3\|4) | FY98 Q (1\|2\|3\|4) | FY99 Q (1\|2\|3\|4) | FY00 Q (1\|2\|3\|4) | FY01 Q (1\|2\|3\|4) | FY02 Q (1\|2) |
|----|-----------|-------|--------|------|------|------|------|------|------|------|
| 1 | Industry Program Brief | 5/7/96 | 5/7/96 | 5/7 ▲ | | | | | | |
| 2 | Industry Discussions | 5/13/96 | 5/14/96 | I | | | | | | |
| 3 | Final Program Solicitation Issued | 5/23/96 | 5/23/96 | 5/23 ▲ | | | | | | |
| 4 | Phase I Proposals Due | 6/25/96 | 6/25/96 | 6/25 ▲ | | | | | | |
| 5 | Phase I Proposal Evaluation | 6/25/96 | 7/9/96 | I | | | | | | |
| 6 | Phase I source selection briefing | 7/10/96 | 7/10/96 | 7/10 ▲ | | | | | | |
| 7 | Phase I Contract Award | 7/11/96 | 7/11/96 | 7/11 ▲ | | | | | | |
| 8 | Phase I Concept Definition | 7/11/96 | 1/9/97 | ■ | | | | | | |
| 9 | Phase II Proposal Due | 11/15/96 | 11/15/96 | | 11/15 ▲ | | | | | |
| 10 | Phase II Functional Design | 1/10/97 | 1/9/98 | | ▬▬▬ | | | | | |
| 11 | Phase III Detail Design, Construction | 1/12/98 | 10/11/00 | | | ▬▬▬▬▬▬ | | | Fleet Evaluation | |
| 12 | Phase IIIb Test Evaluation Planning | 6/30/00 | 10/11/00 | | | | | ■ | | |
| 13 | Phase IV Demonstrations | 10/12/00 | 10/11/01 | | | | | | ▬▬ | |
| 14 | Phase V—Option Exercise | 7/2/01 | 7/6/01 | | | | | | | I |

**Figure 2.1—Arsenal Ship Program Schedule**

The Phase I solicitation added definition to the program. It envisioned that other joint theater assets would perform the Arsenal Ship's command and decision functions, including targeting. The solicitation required the ship's high survivability to be achieved primarily through passive means, and for operating and support costs to be minimized by having either a small crew or none at all. The Cost As an Independent Variable (CAIV) initiative was targeted to the production phase of the program. The solicitation indicated an average Unit Sailaway Price[5] (USP) goal of $450 million for five pro-

---

[5]The USP is for an operational production Arsenal Ship that is fully outfitted and equipped for fleet operations. USP excludes initial support systems costs and programmatic support costs. The ordnance carried by Arsenal Ships is excluded from the program's cost.

duction ships (to be built subsequent to the demonstrator). It established a not-to-exceed USP threshold of $550 million, beyond which the program would be considered unaffordable.

To achieve the USP, the contractors were directed to make whatever performance-versus-cost tradeoffs they deemed necessary. All other capabilities and characteristics of the system were defined as goals; the government did not assert that a system meeting such goals could be demonstrated within the Phase I–IV funding, or produced at an average USP of between $450 and $550 million. The government specifically asked the contractors to determine the capabilities that could be provided within the projected funding, and *demonstrate* that the program could be successfully executed.

The solicitation for Phase I stated the intent to select multiple contractor teams, each of whom would receive an "agreement" funded at $1 million. Six contractor teams responded to the Phase I solicitation. The five awarded agreements for Phase I were:[6]

- General Dynamics, Marine/Bath Iron Works with teammates: General Dynamics, Marine/Electric Boat; Raytheon, Raytheon Electronics Systems; and Science Applications Int'l Corp.

- Hughes Aircraft Co. with teammates: Avondale Shipyards; Advanced Marine Enterprises; Booz•Allen and Hamilton; and McDonnell Douglas

- Lockheed-Martin Government Electronic Systems, with teammates: Litton Industries/Ingalls Shipbuilding; and Newport News Shipbuilding

- Metro Machine Corp., with teammates: Rockwell Int'l/Collins Int'l; Trinity Marine Group; Composite Ships; and Marinex Int'l

- Northrop Grumman Corp. with teammates: National Steel and Shipbuilding Co.; Vitro Corp.; Solipsys; and Band Lavis and Associates, Inc.

---

[6]*Arsenal Ship Program Selects Phase I Contractors*, News Release—Office of Assistant Secretary of Defense (Public Affairs), No. 422-96, 11 July 1996. The sixth was a team led by Seaworthy Systems.

Phase I awards were based on the general criteria below:[7]

- "How well the offeror's Program Solicitation response and proposed Agreement demonstrates an understanding of the Arsenal Ship Capabilities Document (SCD), Arsenal Ship Concept of Operations (CONOPS), Arsenal Ship Program Description and the processes required to execute the program.

- How well the offeror demonstrates its team's capability, experience and resources which will be required to perform the necessary tradeoff studies, design and construct the Arsenal Ship Demonstrator and Arsenal Ships and integrate all necessary systems while maximizing the objectives of the Arsenal Ship program and achieving the USP.

- How well the Integrated Master Schedule depicts a realistic, time-phased plan to achieve the Phase I efforts detailed in the Task Description Document which support meeting of the objectives as contained in the Ship Capabilities Document.

- How well the offeror's proposal addresses or demonstrates the intended use of innovative business and technical concepts which will lead to reductions in cost and schedule throughout the program.

- How well the amount of effort proposed in the Task Description Document for Phase I correlates to the proposed costs for Phase I and provides adequate value to the government."

Phase I, performed during the final quarter of FY96 and first quarter of FY97, was a six-month competitive effort in which the contractor teams performed various tradeoff studies and developed their initial design concept. The Ship Capabilities Document (see Appendix D), Concept of Operations (see Appendix E), and the contractor's own Task Description Document were the guidance for these designs. The contractor teams also developed their Integrated Master Plan (IMP) for all subsequent phases.

---

[7]This list is taken from the *Arsenal Ship Program Solicitation* MDA972-96-R-0001, p. 15.

During Phase I, $1 million in funding was provided to each contractor team with payments based on successful completion of the payable milestones identified as follows:[8]

- Preliminary Program Review completed—30 August 1996

- Life Cycle Cost Parameters Inputs delivered—30 September 1996

- Initial concept design, supporting tradeoff studies, and Integrated Master Plan delivered—15 November 1996

- Preliminary studies of government role in contractor's Integrated Product Team's in Phases II and III delivered—09 January 1997.

## Phase II Solicitation and Description

The down-select to Phase II marked the formal end of Phase I. There was virtually no gap in activities for the contractors between phases, providing continuity uncharacteristic of the traditional process. Data submissions for consideration for Phase II awards began four months into Phase I, at which time the contractor teams provided their formal concept designs for evaluation leading to the Phase II down-select. Oral presentations followed the proposals, providing the opportunity for the government to gain clarification. There was no formal question and answer process, and no Best and Final Offer (BAFO) submissions.[9]

The government's selection process was much quicker, more analytically integrated, and more informative than usual to DARPA and Navy officials. Written proposals were due 15 November 1996. Oral presentations were given during the week of December 4–10. Winners were announced 10 January 1997, less than two months after the original proposals were submitted. In their evaluation process, the ASJPO employed multidisciplinary evaluation teams and called on government experts from the greater Navy acquisition

---

[8]*Arsenal Ship Program Solicitation,* MDA972-96-R-0001, p. 20.

[9]The traditional acquisition process usually includes the submission of initial offers by the contractors, followed by a highly structured question and answer period, followed by a second round of offer submissions. The second round may be what the government defines as the BAFO, or there may be several additional rounds of submissions and Q&As before the government considers the contractor's final offer.

community. The process included cost experts on the technical evaluation teams, and technical experts on the cost-evaluation teams. This tactic provided insight into the contractors' CAIV process, and enabled credible evaluation of their cost estimates. ASJPO officials and their analysis teams directly briefed the decisionmakers. This arrangement circumvented the bureaucracy in the acquisition infrastructure reporting chain. These officials stated that they were provided far more detailed and insightful information than usual.

As in the down-select for Phase I, the Phase II down-select was based on choosing the contractors who would provide the best value. General criteria included how well the team described a credible development program for the Arsenal Ship; the team's description of how its concept demonstrates mission capability while minimizing life-cycle costs, and the team's demonstration of its ability to execute the program (Phases II–V) within cost constraints.[10]

The criteria were not ranked in importance or weighted in any way. The ASJPO stated that they would judge each proposal in its entirety, and that the best overall value would determine the winners. ASJPO personnel described their source selection process as similar to that of a customer choosing a car: They would judge each product by its overall ability to meet the desires of the user for a specified price. The criteria in each of the three elements of the proposal were:

- *Financial approach*: USP methodology and tracking it to the proposed concept design; life-cycle cost methodology, specifically, operating and support cost minimization as a key component of the design; and, Phase II price (value to the government)

- *Management, business, and execution approach*: business approach to meeting the USP; program management structure and production plan; technical, cost, and schedule risk management plan and process; and, quality of proposed Phase II agreement modification (how well it supports the program)

---

[10]Arsenal Ship Program Phase II Downselect Solicitation, MDA972-96-R-0003, 3 October 1996.

- *Technical approach*: concept mission capability within the context of future joint forces; design philosophy that exploits innovative and commercial practices; coherence and clarity of Arsenal Ship Demonstrator and Arsenal Ship design; objectives for the fleet evaluation of the demonstrator; concept design in trade studies, systems design, and design standards; survivability; and, ship operations regarding manning, maintenance, and support.

The government originally intended to select two contractor teams for Phase II, but announced three winners in January 1997:  the General Dynamics, Lockheed Martin, and Northrop Grumman teams. The inclusion of a third design team resulted from the desire to sustain involvement of expertise and technologies unique to that team, providing additional options to the ASJPO for a relatively small additional investment.

Detailed debriefs of the strengths and weaknesses in their proposals were given to all five competitors. The strengths were emphasized to the losing teams; the weaknesses to the winners. This showed the losing teams what aspects of their approach might be useful in future efforts. For the winning teams, the detailed explanation of their proposals' faults got them immediately working in those areas that needed attention. All contractor teams stated that this debrief was the best and most detailed they could remember.

The original agreements with the three winners were modified to cover Phase-II activities. These agreements were to be subsequently modified to include the tasks and funding for future phases. This differs from the traditional acquisition method of issuing a new contract for each program phase, and simplifies moving from phase to phase.

Each contractor team received $15 million via event-payable milestones. For Phase II, the proposed payable milestones schedule was:[11]

- technology development plan delivered—March 1997

---

[11]Actual payable milestones were somewhat different, depending upon the details of each contractor team's amended Agreement.

- program review #1 delivered—May 1997

- interim functional design and software support plan delivered— July 1997

- program review #2 and demonstrator test plan—August 1997

- production plan delivered—October 1997

- functional design and life cycle cost analysis delivered— November 1997.

Two of the Phase-II agreements were signed in January 1997; the third in early February. In April, the program's emphasis was changed, effectively merging the Arsenal Ship and SC 21 programs. The Arsenal Ship Demonstrator was renamed the Maritime Fire Support Demonstrator (MFSD); it was now to serve as the demonstrator for the SC 21 program as well.

During the year-long Phase II effort, each contractor team developed its proposed concept and performance specifications into a functional design. The Arsenal Ship/Maritime Fire Support Demonstrator program was officially canceled on 30 October 1997, just two weeks before contractor proposals were due. DARPA's cancellation letter asked the contractor teams to submit their functional designs and life-cycle cost analyses by 14 November. This completed their Phase-II payable milestones, entitling them to full compensation.

## Phase III Solicitation and Description

The Phase III award process began on 16 June 1997 with the issuance of the first of two planned draft solicitations. The second draft was released 1 August, and the final solicitation on 15 September, as planned. Between each, the ASJPO received questions from the teams, and met individually with each to discuss concerns. These individual discussions would have been illegal under traditional acquisition regulations. The individual meetings focused on proprietary design issues that are not usually discussed in the traditional process. Only generic questions from the individual discussions became public.

Phase III employed a cost-reimbursable type Agreement with an incentive fee structure based upon negotiated cost control and milestone achievements. The winning contractor team's Phase II Agreement would have been modified to include Phase III. The incentive to ensure contractor performance for Phase III linked technical milestones to payments. The competing contractor teams were asked to set both the milestones and payments in their proposed Agreement amendments. The final content of each contractor's proposed Agreement would be negotiated and become part of its Phase III proposal.

This down-select approach deliberately differed from that of the Global Hawk program. Negotiating the final details of the incentive structure before awarding Phase III provided a competitive environment in the process. The government thus gained an upper hand in the negotiations. In the Global Hawk program, the contractor gained the advantage because these details were not negotiated until after the winning team was selected.

## The Balance of the Program Plan

Thi section describes what would have happened had the program not been canceled, and had it followed the plan set out in May 1996. The contractor teams were to provide the government with an "irrevocable offer" to produce five production Arsenal Ships for an average USP of no more than $550 million (FY98 dollars) as part of their Phase III Agreement amendment. A price to convert the demonstrator to the production configuration was also required.

The ASJPO scheduled the Phase III down-select for January 1998. The single Phase III contractor team would have received $389 million (then-year dollars) over a 33-month period to complete a detailed design of both the demonstrator and the production Arsenal Ship, and to construct the demonstrator. The original program rationale, abandoned prior to contractor involvement, considered continuing competition into Phase III, resulting in two demonstrator ships. As in the Global Hawk program, this approach was judged unaffordable.

In Phase IV, DARPA, the Navy, and the contractor team were to conduct a test and evaluation program using the demonstrator, to resolve any risk areas and determine how well the demonstrator satisfied the goals outlined in the Concept of Operations (CONOPS). The contractor team would have planned the test and evaluation, and managed and participated in fleet evaluation. This work may have been performed on a cost-reimbursable basis that would have been negotiated under the contractor team's agreement. The general objective of the phase was the successful demonstration of military utility at an affordable cost. Specific objectives were: Complete a 90-day mission; show connectivity with appropriate Navy assets; prove the ship's passive survivability; and launch ordnance using a remote platform.

If the government elected to exercise the Phase V option, the contractor team would have constructed five Arsenal Ships for the USP defined in the irrevocable offer made at the conclusion of Phase II. Additionally, if the government elected to exercise the conversion option, the contractor team would have converted the demonstrator to the production configuration. The contractor team's agreement, which would have been modified upon acceptance of the irrevocable offer, would have been a fixed-price type with negotiated payment terms.

Had the government chosen to exercise the Phase VI option, the contractor team would have provided all specified service-life support tasks for the Arsenal Ship fleet. Payment terms for this phase would have been negotiated prior to award.

## PROGRAM FUNDING

The cost of the program through design and construction of the demonstrator ship—including all contractor and government activities in Phases I–IV—was set at $520 million (then-year dollars) at program inception.

Table 2.1 shows the original program funding for this portion of the Arsenal Ship program as of the May 1996 MOA between the Navy and DARPA.

As shown in Table 2.2, the Navy added $21 million in funding for a third contractor in Phase II ($15 million for the contractor, and $6 million for additional government activities) in January 1997. These additional funds were added to the Arsenal Ship program budget to preserve the scope and level of effort planned for Phase II.

Table 2.3 shows the final program funding.[12] The appropriation for FY98 was $35 million, but between $18 million and $25 million was reprogrammed to other programs.

---

[12]Navy/DARPA Maritime Fire Support Demonstrator (Arsenal Ship) Program: Issues Arising From Its Termination CRS Report for Congress, 97-1044 F, 10 December 1997.

Table 2.1

Arsenal Ship Program Obligation Plan circa May 1996
(In millions of dollars)

| Phase | | FY96 | FY97 | FY98 | FY99 | FY00 | FY01 | Total |
|---|---|---|---|---|---|---|---|---|
| PHASE I | Navy | $4.0 | | | | | | $4.0 |
| (5 Contractor Teams) | DARPA | $1.0 | | | | | | $1.0 |
| PHASE II | Navy | | $25.0 | | | | | $25.0 |
| (2 Contractor Teams) | DARPA | | $15.0 | | | | | $15.0 |
| PHASE III | Navy | | | $141.0 | $90.0 | $80.0 | | $311.0 |
| (1 Contractor Team) | DARPA | | | $47.0 | $50.0 | $36.0 | | $133.0 |
| PHASE IV | Navy | | | | | | $10.0 | $10.0 |
| (1 Contractor Team) | DARPA | | | | | | $21.0 | $21.0 |
| Total by FY | | $5.0 | $40.0 | $188.0 | $140.0 | $116.0 | $31.0 | $520.0 |

Table 2.2

Arsenal Ship Program Obligation Plan circa January 1997
(In millions of dollars)

| Phase | | FY96 | FY97 | FY98 | FY99 | FY00 | FY01 | Total |
|---|---|---|---|---|---|---|---|---|
| PHASE I (5 Contractor Teams) | Navy | $4.0 | | | | | | $4.0 |
| | DARPA | $1.0 | | | | | | $1.0 |
| PHASE II (3 Contractor Teams) | Navy | | $34.0 | $12.0 | | | | $46.0 |
| | DARPA | | $15.0 | | | | | $15.0 |
| PHASE III (1 Contractor Team) | Navy | | | $91.0 | $140.0 | $80.0 | | $311.0 |
| | DARPA | | | $47.0 | $50.0 | $36.0 | | $133.0 |
| PHASE IV (1 Contractor Team) | Navy | | | | | | $11.0 | $11.0 |
| | DARPA | | | | | | $22.0 | $22.0 |
| Total by FY | | $5.0 | $49.0 | $150.0 | $190.0 | $116.0 | $33.0 | $543.0 |

Table 2.3

Arsenal Ship Program Obligation History circa December 1997
(In millions of dollars)

| Phase | | FY96 | FY97 | FY98 | FY99 | FY00 | FY01 | Total |
|---|---|---|---|---|---|---|---|---|
| PHASE I | Navy | $4.0 | | | | | | $4.0 |
| (5 Contractor Teams) | DARPA | $1.0 | | | | | | $1.0 |
| PHASE II | Navy | | $34.0 | $10–$12 | | | | $44–$46 |
| (3 Contractor Teams) | DARPA | | $15.0 | $0–$5 | | | | $15–$20 |
| PHASE III | Navy | | | | | | | $0 |
| (1 Contractor Team) | DARPA | | | | | | | $0 |
| PHASE IV | Navy | | | | | | | $0 |
| (1 Contractor Team) | DARPA | | | | | | | $0 |
| Total by FY | | $5 | $49 | $10–$17 | $0 | $0 | $0 | $64–$71 |

# Chapter Three

# ARSENAL SHIP ACQUISITION PROCESS

The acquisition strategy for the Arsenal Ship was a radical departure from traditional Navy shipbuilding programs, as well as from traditional Major Defense Acquisition Programs (MDAP).[1] Key attributes of the Arsenal Ship acquisition process included:

- the use of a relatively few broad performance goals in describing desired system capabilities

- giving full design responsibility to the competing contractor teams, and facilitating this by excluding Government Furnished Equipment (GFE) from the program

- a small joint program office

- designating affordability as the only firm requirement, and putting strong emphasis on a small crew

- implementation of Integrated Product and Process Teams (IPPTs)

- structuring the program around DARPA's Section 845 OTA.

We present, in the balance of this chapter, a detailed description of the Arsenal Ship program's acquisition process, followed by a discussion of why the system was not designated an ACTD.

---

[1] *Arsenal Ship Program Selects Phase II Contractors*, Defense News Release, 10 January 1997.

## WEAPON SYSTEM SPECIFICATION

The Ship Capabilities Document (SCD) and CONOPS were the primary documents that drove the design of the Arsenal Ship weapon system concept. The Navy's use of broad descriptions of desired performance, rather than specific requirements, was a major departure from the traditional acquisition approach. These two documents replaced the Mission Need Statement (MNS), Operational Requirements Document (ORD), Analysis of Alternatives (AOA), and Technical Engineering Management Plan (TEMP) usually used.

The SCD and CONOPS outlined the desired capabilities and suggested specific design attributes to provide them. Over a combined length of nine pages[2] (see Appendices D and E), the documents provided minimal performance specifications relative to system design. With few exceptions, the system's characteristics were defined as goals rather than hard requirements. Desired performance was described in broad terms; no specific method for achievement was suggested.

The development of a CONOPS is part of the Air Force's MDAP process, but not part of the Navy's new system development efforts. Air Force CONOPS are far more detailed than the five-page version used in the Arsenal Ship program. The four-page SCD was unique to the Arsenal Ship program. It, in effect, replaced thousands of pages of detailed design specifications that are part of the traditional MDAP process. These two brief documents provided the program's foundation.

The main requirement specified in these documents was to build the ship with the lowest possible development, production, and operating and support costs. The approach was intended to facilitate the lowest possible life-cycle cost by maximizing the contractors' solution space. Broad statements regarding desired performance required each contractor team to develop unique requirements for their weapon system concept. No formal systems specifications existed for the competing contractor teams; as a result, innovative design solutions were expected.

---

[2]Our formatting expands their length.

While this approach is unique for a costly and complex weapon system, similar approaches have been successful in the past. In the early 1970s, the Light Weight Fighter program that resulted in the YF-16 and YF-17 prototype aircraft was based on a one-page statement of work and a two-page statement of desired design and performance characteristics. The winning aircraft from this competitive prototype program became the most prolific fighter jet of our time: the F-16 Falcon. The approach was so successful that the Navy's primary aircraft, the F/A-18 Hornet, came from the losing aircraft's design.

The Global Hawk Tier II+ HAE UAV is a more recent attempt at radically reducing government control of a weapon system's design. Two pages outlined the Global Hawk's mission description and preliminary concept of operations. This ongoing ACTD program was initiated in June 1994. The ASJPO cited the Global Hawk program as the model for the Arsenal Ship's acquisition process.

## CONTRACTOR DESIGN RESPONSIBILITY

The competing contractor teams were responsible for concept design; detailed design and development, including systems integration and software development; and ship production, including combat systems (command and control) and weapon systems (multiple missile types). The design-and-build margins were the contractor's responsibility. The program specified no GFE, forcing the team to provide the system in its entirety.

The process the contractors followed in their design activities began with the SCD/CONOPS, which was the government's only direct contribution. The contractors performed a mission analysis that resulted in various tradeoff studies and ended with a design solution. The contractors then wrote a Ship Requirements Document (SRD) that listed what needed to be done to attain the capability defined in the mission analysis. The SRD led to functional design and allocations that determined the systems to be included, giving the total design solution. The design was subjected to a cost constraint, which provided feedback that often required the SRD to be revised. The entire process was repeated to evolve the design. This is the Total

Ship Systems Engineering (TSSE)[3] approach, in which the contractor's unique specifications (SRD) result in an optimized total system design.

The heavy reliance on the contractor teams during the conceptual design phase, and the transferring of responsibility from the government to the contractors, are both unusual in the context of Navy shipbuilding programs. The traditional acquisition approach does not bring the manufacturing segments of combat systems and shipbuilding industries into the process until later in the development activities. Reliance on industry for the weapon system's design was intended to shorten the timespan between program initiation and operational demonstration, as well as increase design insight and producability.

The approach also enabled the use of commercial practices and off-the-shelf military and commercial components. Giving the contractors total design control from the beginning of the program allowed life-cycle costs to be a primary consideration at the conceptual design phase, when the greatest opportunity exists for cost minimization. Through a shorter design and development cycle, the leveraging of existing components, and total design control, the contractor has the opportunity to reduce dramatically the costs of developing, acquiring, and operating the weapon system.

## Small Joint Program Office

The joint participation by DARPA and the Navy within the program office and the small ASJPO were key aspects to the Arsenal Ship acquisition strategy. Joint program offices are now common, but are usually employed by two or more service branches because each intends to utilize the weapon system of which they are jointly managing the acquisition.

---

[3]TSSE is the process of designing the complete weapon system from a systems engineering perspective. The idea is that the overall architecture dictates the design elements of each of the onboard subsystems. This optimizes weapon system performance, rather than individual subsystem performance as in the traditional Navy acquisition process.

The purpose of joint DARPA/Navy management was for the Navy to take advantage of DARPA business practices in general, DARPA's Section 845 OTA[4] specifically, and the OTA program management experience DARPA accumulated in the two years prior to the inception of the program. The purpose of the joint program office was to facilitate the acquisition process; normally, its purpose would have been to ensure that the weapon system meets the requirements of the multiple services for which it is being procured.

The memorandum establishing the Arsenal Ship program specified a maximum of nine staff members for the ASJPO, an unprecedented number for a program expected to cost billions.[5] The total onsite staff, including Systems Engineering Technical Assistance (SETA) contractor personnel, peaked in the spring of 1997 at 20. Weapon system program offices managed under the MDAP process are typically staffed by 200–400 persons.[6] Even in the case of a program managed under special circumstances, such as the F-117 Nighthawk or the HAE UAV Global Hawk, program office staffs run two to four dozen persons.[7]

The ASJPO's role was intentionally limited compared to that of a program office for a traditional MDAP. Government interaction with contractors fundamentally changed, requiring cultural adjustments within the contractor teams and the program office. The streamlined acquisition strategy and reliance on the contractors for design responsibility made the small size of the ASJPO feasible. The absence of overt oversight eliminated activities and the personnel to perform them from both the contractor teams and the ASJPO. The ASJPO provided de facto oversight informally through its daily participation in the team's activities. The small program office size

---

[4]At the time of the Arsenal Ship program's inception (March 1996), only DARPA had Section 845 authority. Section 804 of the FY97 National Defense Authorization Act amended Section 845, expanding the authority to the military departments and other components of the DoD.

[5]The subsequent MOA specified that DARPA, NAVSEA, and Office of Naval Research (ONR) each initially provide two billets, growing to three as the program proceeded.

[6]*Application of F-117 Acquisition Strategy to Other Programs in the New Acquisition Environment,* RAND MR-749-AF, 1996.

[7]Ibid.; *The Global Hawk Unmanned Aerial Vehicle Acquisition Process—A Summary of Phase I Experience,* RAND MR-809-DARPA, 1997.

also limited technical exchange, thus encouraging industry innovation without influencing the design approach or pressuring the contractors into design choices through ASJPO opinions.

## UNIT SAILAWAY PRICE, NONRECURRING FUNDING, AND SMALL CREW

The Arsenal Ship program mandated one firm requirement from the beginning—the $450-million USP goal, with an absolute ceiling of $550 million. However, two additional "requirements" quickly became apparent. The winning contractor for Phase III would receive $405 million total funding for the first three phases of the program. This funding was described from the outset as firm; the contractor team would complete these phases within the stated funding. In addition, the weapon system configuration was to be designed with a crew complement of no more than 50. Even though the original program documents emphasized the single requirement, they included the two additional "requirements," stating clearly from the beginning that they were of great importance.

As previously discussed, the government established the USP requirement for the Arsenal Ship fleet planned to be built in Phase V. The USP is defined as "the average unit price of five Arsenal Ships, calculated in FY98 base year dollars."[8] This affordability constraint is similar to that of the Global Hawk and DarkStar HAE UAVs. The acquisition plan for each of these UAV types called for an average Unit Flyaway Price (UFP) of $10 million for air vehicles 11–20. In the Arsenal Ship program, the government stated a USP goal as well as a not-to-exceed USP threshold, beyond which the program could be canceled. The $100 million USP difference between the goal and threshold in the program was meant to provide flexibility in developing the best value system. This cost flexibility was not offered to the HAE UAV developers.

Total planned funding for the development and demonstration phases of the Arsenal Ship program (Phases I–IV) was $520 million in then-year dollars. This funding was intended to cover all nonrecurring design and development costs, the construction of the demon-

---

[8]Arsenal Ship Program Solicitation MDA972-96-R-0001, 23 May 1996.

strator ship, and operational evaluation using the demonstrator. The contractor chosen to build the demonstrator would deliver that ship, ready for operational evaluation, for the previously stated total price of $405 million—$1 million Phase I funding; $15 million Phase II funding; and, $389 million Phase III funding.[9]

The design, development, and production of the demonstrator and production Arsenal Ships were to be conducted under a CAIV approach.[10] Whatever could be accomplished within the available funding would define the program's content. The initial Arsenal Ship Program Solicitation explicitly stated that the government did not know whether the desired system capability could be achieved within the USP. The contractor teams had to demonstrate that the capabilities could be attained, or come as close as possible within the USP constraint. This willingness to trade performance for cost was also patterned after the HAE UAV program.

The final "requirement" was also aimed at minimizing cost. The small crew size was designated because personnel costs are usually the largest component of a ship's operating costs. Surface combatants of the size and complexity of the Arsenal Ship usually have crews numbering in the hundreds.[11] Designing an Arsenal Ship with a crew of 50 or fewer required nontraditional design concepts and use of the best technology available in the commercial ship-building industry.[12]

The lack of detailed weapon system specifications, and the transferral of complete design responsibility to the contractor at the beginning, enabled the unprecedented affordability and crew size. Use of the traditional Navy acquisition approach would have substantially determined the design of the lead and follow-on ships even before

---

[9]The differences between the $405 million for the winning contractor and the total program funding of $520 million shown in Table 2.1 are government activity funding for Phases I–IV; funding provided to the losing contractors in Phases I and II; and, contractor funding for Phase IV.

[10]Joint Memorandum: ARSENAL SHIP PROGRAM, March 18, 1996. See Appendix F.

[11]See Appendix C for comparative systems. The initial Navy estimate for the Arsenal Ship concept's crew using conventional Navy billeting was 269.

[12]For a thorough discussion of the application of commercial ship design aspects, see Appendix B.

the prime system contractor was brought into the process. Because of the detailed systems specifications and the GFE provided to the contractor, the Navy's ship costs using the traditional process are a "fall out" from the accepted design. The fundamental difference in approaches is that, in the Arsenal Ship program, the funding drove the design solution; typically, the design solution drives the funding.

## INTEGRATED PRODUCT AND PROCESS TEAMS

The memorandum establishing the Arsenal Ship Program specified that ASJPO personnel would be part of an industry-government team that worked with contractor personnel to achieve the program objectives. The Phase I solicitation indicates that the contractor teams would conduct a study evaluating what the government's involvement in the contractor's Integrated Product Teams (IPT) would be in subsequent phases, and set up an integrated management framework to facilitate the IPT[13] philosophy during those phases.

The contractor's use of IPPTs was vital to use of the TSSE design approach, and for implementation of the CAIV process to stay within the limited developmental phase funding and meet the USP. The use of IPPT with government representation promoted integrated design solutions while affording the government the insight—rather than traditional oversight—required for confidence that the contractor was progressing. The IPPT management approach allows the government and contractor team to work together in determining the best design while providing the most capability within affordability constraints.

The use of IPPT represents a major cultural and procedural change in the acquisition process. In the traditional Navy ship-design approach, the ship systems, combat systems, and hull are designed substantially independently of each other. The organizations re-

---

[13]IPT can stand for Integrated Product Team or Integrated Process Team. For an integrated product team, systems-oriented and functionally integrated teams are formed, each focusing on a given part of the weapon system and each including all relevant functional specialties such as support and user representatives. For integrated process teams, process-oriented and functionally integrated teams are formed, each focusing on a process required for the successful development or production of the weapon system and including all relevant functional specialties.

sponsible for these designs operate in a traditional "stovepipe" mode. When the lead ship is built, the prime contractor must integrate the various pieces of the weapon system. This approach works, but is far from optimal from both cost and functionality standpoints. The problem with the approach is that the systems comprising the overall weapon system are not designed with an overall integrated architecture in mind.

## SECTION 845 OTHER TRANSACTIONS AUTHORITY

Title 10 USC 2371 provides authority to the Secretary of Defense, the Director of DARPA, and the military departments to enter into "other transactions" outside the traditional acquisition regulations—the Other Transactions Authority (OTA). Section 845 of the FY94 Defense Authorization Act extends the OTA, on a pilot basis,[14] to prototype programs that are directly relevant to a weapons system proposed for the DoD.

The OTA is not defined, except perhaps in the negative, in that it is not a standard procurement contract, grant, or cooperative agreement. It is therefore not subject to the laws, rules, and regulations that govern these instruments.[15] The OTA allows DARPA to conduct what amounts to experiments with the acquisition process,[16] and provides the freedom to tailor each program to a degree not possible in the traditional acquisition process. The ASJPO characterized OTA as de facto deregulation of acquisition.

The OTA allows DARPA to conduct technology demonstrations and prototype projects using nonprocurement contracts. The OTA can be used even if a standard contract would be appropriate or feasible. It allows for the use of inherently flexible "Agreements" that are far simpler than traditional contracts. These Agreements enable tailor-

---

[14]The period of this authority has subsequently been extended through 30 September 1999.

[15]*Aerospace America*, September 1997, "Other Applications for Other Transactions," p. 35.

[16]Stated by the Hon. Paul Kaminski, Under Secretary of Defense for Acquisition and Technology. Given before the Subcommittee on Acquisition and Technology of the Senate Armed Services Committee, 20 March 1996.

ing of the contracting process to each project, rather than the reverse.

DARPA intended the approach to shorten development times, enhance weapon system affordability, and help focus the government and contractors on objectives rather than compliance with acquisition regulations. The OTA allows DARPA to implement streamlined acquisition procedures such as Generally Accepted Accounting Practices, rather than the more-convoluted Government Cost Accounting Standards. The OTA requires compliance with applicable fiscal and socioeconomic laws,[17] but allows departure from acquisition-specific laws and regulations, including the Armed Services Procurement Act, CICA, FAR, and DFARS. Existing DoD practices, regulations, directives, MILSPECS, etc. need not apply. In 1994 DARPA used its OTA to facilitate the Agreement used as a contracting mechanism for the Global Hawk HAE UAV program in a manner similar to that for the Arsenal Ship program.

The ASJPO utilized the OTA along with a unique and nonbureaucratic implementation of DoD Directive 5000.1.[18] This combination gave the contractors considerable flexibility to use innovative business and program management practices. They were allowed to retain data rights and patent rights, and could choose their own reporting system or management process. Commercial or DoD processes for quality, reliability, systems engineering, etc., were acceptable.

One of the primary goals of this approach was to increase the number of private sector firms participating in projects, thus providing greater opportunities to leverage commercial technologies. The competitive base was expanded because a significant barrier to market entry—institutionalized military processes—was removed. Two contractor teams bidding for Phase I awards included firms that would not usually bid on a Naval surface combatant weapon system

---

[17]Specifically: appropriations law regarding what dollars can be used, and Title VI of the Civil Rights Act of 1964 as amended (42 U.S.C. 2000-d).

[18]"Defense Acquisition," 15 March 1996. DoD Directive 5000.1 states the policies and principles for all DoD acquisition programs, establishing a disciplined but flexible management approach for acquiring quality products that satisfy the user's needs.

(Metro Machine and Seaworthy Systems); ironically, both were eliminated from the program by Phase II.

The OTA was the cornerstone of the entire Arsenal Ship acquisition process.  It directly enabled the use of a relatively few broad performance characteristics, and the assignment of full design responsibility to the competing contractor teams.  These two facets, in turn, made possible the small program office, the design conceived to accommodate the affordability constraints, and the effective implementation of the IPPT management approach.

## WHY NOT AN ADVANCED CONCEPT TECHNOLOGY DEMONSTRATOR?

At first glance, one might expect that the Arsenal Ship program was an ACTD.  The program met many of the criteria, and the characteristics of the program management and acquisition strategy were similar to existing ACTDs (e.g. HAE UAV).  The program was in fact managed outside both the MDAP and ACTD processes, which are the mainstream acquisition approaches currently employed.

The Arsenal Ship program's scope and structure were determined before the program formally existed.  DARPA, the Navy, and OSD decided to manage the program outside of the ACTD process.  This resulted in an unprecedented opportunity to tailor management to the unique characteristics of the program.  ASJPO officials commented that the ACTD process imposes constraints that would hinder use of the innovative acquisition process that was employed in the Arsenal Ship program.

Had the Arsenal Ship program been an ACTD, it would have been the Class II type.[19]  Upon completion, Class II ACTD products are expected to enter into Low Rate Initial Production (LRIP), sometimes with development activities preceding LRIP.  The Arsenal Ship program plan was a complete weapon-system acquisition, in that it included all production articles envisioned by the Navy.  ACTD programs are expected to have a duration of two to four years.  The de-

---

[19]There are three classes of ACTDs:  Class I—Information systems with special-purpose software operating on commercial workstations; Class II—weapon or sensor systems; and, Class III—system of systems.

velopment and operational demonstration phases of the program (Phases I–IV) were scheduled to take slightly more than five years. Because Phases V and VI included the production of the proposed Arsenal Ship fleet as well as contractor support of the fleet throughout its life, the program's planned content and duration went far beyond the scope of a Class II ACTD.

A second and equally important reason for the Arsenal Ship's unique acquisition approach was its funding requirements. Phase V alone called for the production of five ships and the modification of the demonstrator, at a projected cost of almost $3 billion. At the time of program inception, the planned funding for Phase III in FY98 was $188 million, which is beyond the scope of almost all ACTDs (with the exception of the HAE UAV program).[20] In addition, no production funding is customarily planned for ACTD programs.

---

[20]FY96 and FY97 funding for the 10 ACTDs listed in the Advanced Concept Technology Demonstrator Master Plan dated April 1995 averages $70 million per year per ACTD. The most funding any one program receives in a single year is $190 million, for the HAE UAV.

# Chapter Four

# A CONTRAST OF ACQUISITION APPROACHES

To better explain and interpret the effects of the innovative and nontraditional acquisition procedures applied in the Arsenal Ship program, we outline traditional acquisition process approaches for Navy ships, the differences in the Arsenal Ship approach, and the schedule implications of these differences. Appendix C provides an in-depth comparison and analysis of the cost and schedule differences between the traditional Navy approach and that planned for the Arsenal Ship program.

## THE TRADITIONAL NAVY PROCESS

Listed below is the sequence of events currently employed in the Navy's ship design and build process for acquisitions falling under the MDAP designation as Acquisition Category (ACAT) I programs. Activities prior to Milestone I have differed over the past 20 years, but the events characterizing the current process, and the elapsed calendar time associated with these events, are substantially unchanged. The process can be outlined as follows:

- development of an MNS, ORD, and AOA

- begin concept design and feasibility studies, usually designated Milestone 0

- begin Preliminary and Contract Design, usually designated Milestone I

- begin Engineering and Manufacturing Development (EMD) and contract-letting for detailed design and lead-ship production, usually designated Milestone II

- follow-on production authorization and contract-letting.

The Navy's traditional acquisition approach begins with requirements development. Programs that are expected to cost billions of dollars are subjected to a detailed justification process before steps are actually taken to design and build the system. The first step is to write an MNS. This document explains what mission the new system will perform, and why the mission is required. From the MNS, an ORD is developed. This describes what, in operational terms, the system must do to accomplish its mission. Then a detailed AOA is prepared, analyzing the various ways of accomplishing the mission and determining if the acquisition of a new weapon system is warranted. Once these justifying documents have been approved by acquisition and requirements decisionmakers, the Navy writes a detailed system specification.

The next step in the traditional process is the development of the concept, followed by the preliminary designs. The Navy may separate concept and preliminary designs because several distinct concepts may be explored to accomplish a mission. The Navy has traditionally relied on their large internal design group for both concept design and preliminary design. This group conducts tradeoff studies between multiple candidate concepts, and maximizes the utility of its preferred design.

Contract design efforts yield a design sufficiently detailed to facilitate the definition of a contract to build the vessel. For Naval vessels, the contract design will be developed once the acquisition decisionmakers have approved the preliminary design. The Navy usually completes the contract design, but in recent years design agents or shipyards have been employed as consultants.

The Navy then takes its contract design and develops an RFP on which the shipyards will bid. The RFP calls for the detailed design and construction of the lead ship, and often includes options for the initial follow-on ships. The RFP typically consists of multiple volumes, and requires a 60-day proposal effort from the contractors; it also usually costs each contractor millions of dollars to complete. A question and answer period follows the proposal submissions. This customarily results in a revised RFP from the government, requiring another proposal from the contractors. Eventually, a BAFO is requested from the contractors, and the government selects a winner. The entire process often takes more than six months, and has taken up to two years in extreme circumstances.

The government generally determines the winner on a best-value basis, awarding the contract to the firm that delivers the most cost-effective design solution meeting the specified system performance. The contractors do not have the opportunity to trade performance for cost. Although a rigorous cost estimation and analysis proposal is required, overruns requiring additional funding are common.

Follow-on production occurs as the government exercises options in the lead-ship contract award, or when separate contracts are issued. The government often awards follow-on production contracts to a second and even a third shipyard, if funding is available and the production quantity merits it. This use of multiple sources adds competition to the procurement phase, forcing the contractor to control costs or risk losing future business.

## ARSENAL SHIP PROCESS DIFFERENCES

DARPA and the Navy shortened and simplified the process dramatically in the Arsenal Ship program. They eliminated the steps of developing and obtaining approval of the MNS, ORD, and AOA. Both an SCD and CONOPS were developed, but these documents were kept simple and short, and were not required to go through the usual layered approval procedures. The contractor teams were completely responsible for satisfying the CONOPS and SCD.

The Arsenal Ship Phase I activity constituted the concept definition process. Phase II activity constituted the equivalent of both the preliminary and contract design activities. Competition in Phase II, the affordability emphasis throughout the program, and the contractor's ownership of the system's specification combined to provide the government with more options, a better value, and better insight by the contractors into the system's design. In addition, all this was accomplished in much less time than within the traditional shipbuilding approach. The Arsenal Ship program planned to select a single contractor team for Phase III, under a competitive source-selection process. This approach allowed a choice between three completely different designs, rather than substantively identical concepts required by the highly specified traditional process.

Phase IV required the theater Commanders-in-Chief (CINCs) to operate the weapon system with the fleet and make a determination of its military utility *before* a commitment was made for follow-on production. In the traditional approach, the Navy ratifies a commitment to follow-on production—and multiple vessels are usually already being built—before the lead ship even undergoes sea trials, much less fleet operations.

Phase V would have occurred only at the government's discretion. If the theater CINCs found sufficient military utility in the demonstrator, and the Navy supported continued production, then the DoD could take the production option to the authorizing and appropriation committees and Congress. Then, the same contractor team that built the demonstrator would have built all the production Arsenal Ships, thus excluding competing shipyards. According to the program plan, competition for the production phase occurred in Phases I and II, and was manifested in the USP irrevocable offer made at the conclusion of Phase II.

## SCHEDULE COMPARISON TO THE DDG 51 PROGRAM

The Guided Missile Destroyer program designated the DDG 51 provides the best schedule comparison for developmental activities to the Arsenal Ship program. The DDG 51 Arleigh Burke-class program began in 1980; thus, its acquisition process is representative of the Navy's traditional way of acquiring a new surface combatant. The DDG 51 is a smaller and more complex vessel than what was envisioned as an Arsenal Ship, but in a technical sense the DDG 51 is the best possible comparison.

The DDG 51 is a general purpose, multimission destroyer. Much like the envisioned Arsenal Ship, it conducts surface-strike and fire-support missions using TOMAHAWK antiship and land attack missiles, HARPOON missiles, and a large caliber gun. The DDG 51 also carries the Navy Standard Missile for self-protection, as was envisioned for the Arsenal Ship. Both ship types were to operate in an environment with threats from the air, surface, and subsurface.

The DDG 51 accomplished a major technological achievement for its time, being the first surface combatant to host a truly integrated combat system, the AEGIS Weapon System. The Arsenal Ship, through its remote launch capability and unprecedented connectivity with DoD-wide force elements, would have boasted a similar technological achievement. In both programs, these groundbreaking capabilities were based on the evolution of existing subsystems.

Comparing the time of demonstrator delivery in the Arsenal Ship program to that of the lead ship in the DDG 51 program is appropriate in a technical maturity sense. At the beginning of the Arsenal Ship program, the only significant difference envisioned between the demonstrator and the production configuration was Vertical Launch System (VLS) depopulation, implying a completely developed system. The planned "completeness" of the demonstrator being degraded by the second half of Phase II was caused by a projected shortfall in Phase III funding, not by a schedule complication.

In another sense, the validity of the comparison is questionable. The DDG 51 data are actuals, whereas the Arsenal Ship program was not executed beyond Phase II; thus, its scheduled duration for Phase III is purely projected. In the DDG 51 program, no delivery date for the lead ship was estimated until December 1988, about two years before the ship's planned delivery. That initial estimate proved accurate; the ship was delivered only two months later than anticipated. The DDG 51 program experience does not provide guidance as to how much the delivery date of the Arsenal Ship demonstrator might have slipped.

The development schedules of the two programs are compared in Figure 4.1. The Arsenal Ship acquisition approach, from program inception through demonstrator or "lead ship" delivery, was planned for significantly less than half the time required by the DDG 51 program. Note that the Arsenal Ship demonstrator was to be delivered just two months (in elapsed time) after the DDG 51 program Detailed Design and Lead Ship Construction contract was awarded.

In the Arsenal Ship program, most of the activities for developing the SCD and CONOPS happened between mid-March and early May

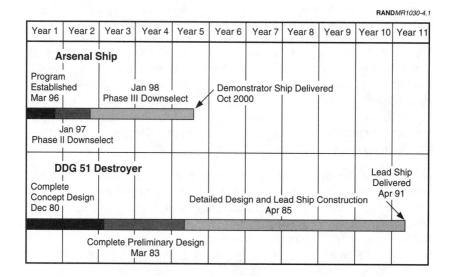

**Figure 4.1—Early Development Program Schedule Comparison**

1996, the two months between program initiation and the release of the Phase I solicitation. Scheduled completion for Phases I–III was about 51 months, with the delivery of the demonstrator in 2000. The total elapsed time from program inception to demonstrator ship delivery was to be just four and one-half years.

The Concept Design for the DDG 51 class was completed in December 1980.[1] Adding the calendar time from program inception through the concept design phase would make the comparison to the planned Arsenal Ship program more accurate, and would increase the duration of the DDG 51's developmental process. The Preliminary and Contract Designs were completed in March 1983 and June 1984, respectively. Detailed Design and Lead Ship Contract Award occurred in April 1985. The lead ship was delivered in April 1991, more than 10 years after Concept Design completion.

---

[1]Data on the DDG 51 are taken from the program Selected Acquisition Reports (SARs) dated December 1982 through December 1991. Information regarding activities prior to the completion of the Concept Design is not included in the program history covered in these SARs.

# Chapter Five

# ACQUISITION PROGRAM AND PROCESS IMPRESSIONS

A series of interviews produced our impressions of the program structure and acquisition process. We tried to capture the experience of, and obtain feedback from, the ASJPO and contractor teams regarding their involvement in the program. We asked for comments on key attributes of the acquisition process. We asked the ASJPO how the contractor teams were responding to the acquisition approach, and vice versa. We also asked for opinions on how they expected the program to unfold in future phases. Our interviews revealed differences in perceptions of the strategy between the competing contractor teams and between the ASJPO and the contractors. We also noted changing opinions on both sides as the program progressed.

## INTERVIEWS

We conducted three sets of interviews with ASJPO personnel. The first was conducted shortly after the completion of Phase I and focused on its events. We conducted the second about midway through Phase II, at which time the program's original schedule and plan were still in place. By that point, it had become clear that the program was in danger of not receiving sufficient FY98 funding. We wanted to capture the activities of Phase II and the mindset of the program office staff before the program changed as a result of the looming shortfall. We conducted the final set of interviews shortly after the program was officially terminated, and focused on the program office's insights into the cancellation. Each set of interviews took one to two days, and in each case we met with between four and eight ASJPO members.

The contractors interviewed and the dates of the interviews are listed in Table 5.1. We conducted two sets of interviews with the contractor teams. The first took place in late 1996, after the contractors submitted their Phase II written and oral proposals, but prior to the downselect. We interviewed four of the five contractor teams awarded Phase I Agreements. The fifth declined to participate at the time the others were interviewed, though we were granted a subsequent phone interview.

The second set of interviews took place in December 1997, after the program had been canceled and the contractors had submitted their final deliverables completing their Phase II commitment. The three Phase II contractor teams participated. In our interviews in both program phases, we generally met for several hours with a few members of the lead firm(s) of each contractor team.

## ORGANIZATION OF MATERIAL

We divide the information gathered from these interviews into two areas: *aspects* of the acquisition program and process, and specific *issues* arising throughout the program's execution. We discuss the latter in Chapter Six.

### Table 5.1

### Contractor Interviews

| Contractor Team | First Interview Date | Second Interview Date |
|---|---|---|
| Hughes/Avondale | 9 December 1996 | N/A |
| Northrop Grumman | 10 December 1996 | 3 December 1997 |
| Lockheed Martin/ Newport News | 11 December 1996 | 16 December 1997 |
| General Dynamics Marine/Raytheon | 12 December 1996 | 17 December 1997 |
| Metro Machine | declined; brief 25 February 1997 phone discussion | N/A |

The information acquired in the interviews does not lend itself to discussion by *attribute* as described in Chapter Three. The program structure described in Chapter Two enters into our discussion of some of the aspects discussed below. The aspects of the acquisition program and process discussed relate to the attributes described in Chapter Three, but in a convoluted way. Each aspect, and how it ties into the material from Chapters Two and Three, is listed below.

- Section 845 OTA and Acquisition Waivers:  As discussed in Chapter Three, the OTA and associated acquisition waivers granted the Arsenal Ship program facilitated many of the program's other unique process attributes.  For this reason, we discuss the OTA implication first.

- Performance Requirements and Contractor Design Responsibility: We discussed weapon-system specification and contractor design responsibility separately in Chapter Three. Here we combine them because, in practice, they were implemented as one.

- Program Structure:   Development Phases Funding and Schedule—The program structure discussion herein incorporates contractor and ASJPO insights of the program overview, which follows the material in Chapter Two.  We also discuss funding for Non-Recurring Engineering (NRE) efforts in Phases I–III, which is a part of the USP, NRE, and small crew size discussion in Chapter Three.

- Unit Sailaway Price: We handle the USP individually here, as opposed to Chapter Three where it is grouped with the USP, NRE, and small crew size. The USP applies to Phase V of the program. This separated it from the others that were of more immediate concern to both the program office and the contractors.

- Contractor Teaming and Business Arrangements: The arrangements employed by the contractors were a function of the program structure described in Chapter Two, and the design responsibility, requirements, IPPT, and OTA attributes described in Chapter Three.

- Interactions between the Contractor Teams, ASJPO, and other government offices: These interactions resulted from the design responsibility, small joint program office, IPPT, and OTA discussions in Chapter Three. We include information about material regarding interaction with other government organizations that affected the program.

## SECTION 845 OTA AND ACQUISITION WAIVERS

The ASJPO took advantage of the OTA not only to free itself from the confines of DoD Instruction 5000.2-R,[1] but to exploit fully the inherent flexibility of DoD Directive 5000.1. The OTA allowed the ASJPO to build the program around the goal of having the contractors demonstrate the *operational* performance of the weapon system— meeting the SCD and CONOPS—instead of demonstrating *engineering* performance in the form of detailed specifications.

The contractor teams explicitly stated that the streamlined process allowed them to save a lot of money. One source of cost savings, both in Phases I and II and expected in subsequent phases, was from the use of the contractor's accounting, planning, reporting, and management systems and formats as opposed to government-imposed systems. The absence of oversight functions and their associated personnel brought additional savings.

The ASJPO felt they were able to implement the spirit of DoD Directive 5000.1 without being constrained by traditional acquisition procedures. They stated that turning over design control to the contractor teams does not require Section 845 OTA in a legal sense. Industry could be given design responsibility under the traditional process; culturally, however, that would be difficult to execute. The OTA provided the Arsenal Ship program made it "all right" with the greater Navy community for the contractors to have this control.

An additional advantage cited by the program office was the high visibility of the OTA, and the resulting quick access to senior decisionmakers. This empowered the contractors to meet the compressed schedule.

---

[1]"Mandatory Procedures for Major Defense Acquisition Programs and Major Automated Information Systems," 1996.

## Phase I

At the conclusion of Phase I, all of the teams stated that they would have bid on the program even if it were conducted under more traditional acquisition processes. However, they acknowledged a general feeling of empowerment as a result of the innovative process employed. In general, the contractor teams felt that the freedom to manage their programs using common sense, and the freedom to set their own priorities and engage in the highest value-added activities (in their minds) as a result of Section 845 OTA, were among the most valuable elements of the program and key to its perceived success. Some teams found benefit in the improved access to the ASJPO, laboratories, and users that the process provided.

Those teams led by prime contractors who did not consider themselves traditional Naval surface combatant contractors had an additional reason to be pleased with the DARPA-led effort. They feared that a Navy-led program might have resulted in a bias against them because of their lack of experience in surface combatant design and construction. One of these teams survived into Phase II. In this regard, the DARPA-led program using Section 845 authority appears to have had a positive effect in heightening a sense of fair competition.

## Phase II

The open communications and one-on-one meetings during the solicitation and proposal process that the OTA made possible gratified both the contractor teams and ASJPO. In these discussions, proprietary design issues were aired while in the proposal stage, allowing each contractor to target the government's concerns before their final proposal was submitted.

Midway through Phase II, the ASJPO also described the OTA as "common sense acquisition." They described the OTA as minimizing barriers between industry and government, thus providing win–win solutions. Because the OTA was used to render irrelevant all protest provisions in the Federal Air Regulation (FAR), all legal barriers to open communication were removed. This provided ASJPO/contractor relationships described by the ASJPO as "liberating."

Each team's concepts were used in an operational simulation exercise in China Lake During Phase II. This gave them a chance to see how their concept would interact with other joint-force assets, and how the CINCs would use them. The purpose was to assist the contractors in understanding the types of activities the Navy might employ in Phase IV to assess the operational utility of each contractor's unique Arsenal Ship design. This early user involvement during the preliminary or functional design stage was a unique program aspect that took direct advantage of the great process flexibility afforded by the OTA.

One ASJPO member we interviewed midway through Phase II speculated that the only problem with the OTA was that it created an apparent "fear" in Congress. The lack of congressional oversight and Congress's inability to reallocate funds to facilitate other agendas could create such a fear. These Congressional prerogatives are part of the traditional defense program acquisition process.

## PERFORMANCE REQUIREMENTS AND CONTRACTOR DESIGN RESPONSIBILITY

The ASJPO considered the absence of detailed requirements and the transfer of design responsibility to the contractor teams the most striking aspects of the acquisition approach. These strategies required cultural changes within the contractor teams and the program office. The contractors had to learn to develop their own system specifications and make cost-performance trade decisions regarding the relative importance of various design aspects. The program office had to resist its inclination to provide direction to the contractors regarding both the relative importance of system capabilities and the design solutions that would provide them.

### Phase I

The ASJPO felt that about six weeks of Phase I had elapsed before the contractors understood the depth of their design responsibility and authority. Some teams were still in the process of adjusting to their increased autonomy and responsibility at the end of Phase I. All of the contractor teams stated that they either felt comfortable from the beginning, or eventually became comfortable, with the way in which performance was specified for the Arsenal Ship, and their responsibility for developing the system concept that would provide that performance.

The flexibility provided by the absence of detailed hard requirements, and the relegation of those requirements to subcontractors, gave the contractors more flexibility to tailor system concepts through design tradeoffs than a traditional approach affords. Some of the contractor teams were slow to realize that the ASJPO was serious about not providing additional detail or indicating preferred directions. All felt that this new and unusual approach was beneficial.

The contractor teams had adopted concept designs by the end of Phase I that provided levels of performance and key system attributes as detailed in the SCD and CONOPS, with few exceptions. The proposed designs and level of technical risk inherent to the competing teams' concepts were quite disparate. All of the competitors were convinced they could provide an operational ship with a crew smaller than the threshold of 50, with most coming in at around half that number. One team believed its design could be operated completely by remote control, requiring no crew.

## Phase II

In Phase II, the contractors stated that they took full advantage of their control over design, rapidly evolving their designs to support both the TSSE concept and the CAIV design emphasis. They stated that they strongly preferred this method to the traditional process. The loose specification of performance goals provided them the leeway required to propose truly innovative designs. They steadfastly followed the CAIV design approach, with some requiring their detail design engineers to address costs directly.

Their concepts included both modified commercial hull designs and innovative hull forms; incorporation of the best ship systems technology available in the commercial sector; and low observable technologies from their aircraft, submarine, and other product lines. The designs incorporated significant new developments, including conformal antennae, damage control systems, and vertical launch systems. Crew sizes remained about the same as Phase I expectations, averaging 22 persons. The small crew sizes were attained through the direct integration of hull, mechanical, and electrical systems with onboard combat systems, and redundancy providing high reliability with minimal under-way maintenance. The contractor team that proposed operating with no crew eventually determined that this approach was not cost effective, proposing a crew size consistent with their competitors' designs. A different competitor that had not previously proposed a remote-controlled design claimed its evolved design could operate in a high-threat environment for a short time without a crew.

According to the ASJPO, the industry teams continued to adjust to their design responsibility during Phase II. ASJPO said the contractors were responding well to the trade-space flexibility afforded them by the process, and noted that all teams had adopted a systems-engineering design approach. The teams were truly thinking "out of the box" in terms of technical design. In many instances, standard Navy design solutions were abandoned in favor of commercial technologies. The program office was pleased with the proposed applications.

Because the industry teams were given full design responsibility, the ASJPO could not control design decisions that may have been motivated by contractor agendas inconsistent with those of the program. The contractors could allocate resources however they saw fit. In Phase II, all three heavily invested in new VLS designs, which are arguably not required to demonstrate the Arsenal Ship concept—the existing MK 41 could be used. One possible explanation for these investments was that the contractors believed they could sell their new VLS to the government for the SC 21 and other Navy vessels more readily than they could sell Arsenal Ships.

Some teams reportedly had difficulty getting newly added staff to accept the challenge of the innovative process. This is not surprising, given that the contractor team staffs numbered about 50 for Phase I, and increased to over 200 in Phase II. The program office also stated that the teams had taken very different approaches to their design process—one was innovative, another traditional, and the third somewhere in-between. The contractors reportedly handled their software development approaches the same way.

One area where the contractors could not be given direct control was the offboard systems intended to task the Arsenal Ship remotely. To integrate these assets into the program, the ASJPO set up the Arsenal Ship Offboard Systems (ASOS) working group. Affected offboard system program offices were asked to provide representatives. The group met every four to six weeks to facilitate communications between program offices, improve understanding of the CONOPS, and be apprised of the program's status. Members from intermediate management and technical ranks generally served. The technical representatives were described as the more supportive.

## PROGRAM STRUCTURE: DEVELOPMENT PHASES FUNDING AND SCHEDULE

### Phase I

At the end of Phase I, the ASJPO stated that from program inception they fully expected the contractors to add significant funding to the $1 million provided. The contractor teams reported that they obtained substantial corporate support (funding) for Phase I, spending on average about $5 million. They also anticipated that major corporate support would be needed for Phase II should they survive the down-select. The program office knew that Phase II would cost each contractor roughly twice the $15 million provided.

The ASJPO also knew that Phase III was underfunded, and that the winning Phase III contractor would have to omit systems from the demonstrator to keep costs within that phase's $389 million funding. The contractors agreed that Phase III was underfunded, but appeared confident that either the funding would be increased or that they could invoke their design control to fit the available funding.

At the end of Phase I, the ASJPO felt that both Phases I and II were too short. They felt Phase I should have been about nine months, and Phase II about 18 months. The effective length of Phase I was just over four months,[2] which ASJPO noted as too short to process a

---

[2]The contractors were required to submit their written proposals for Phase II on 15 November 1996, slightly over four months after their Phase I contract awards on 10 July. Phase II oral proposals to the ASJPO were in early December, but only material included in the written proposals was allowed to be presented.

mission analysis, derive performance requirements, develop major design options, and get a reasonable understanding of the USP. As a consequence, these processes were done in parallel; the results provided were inconsistent or lacked depth. The ASJPO pointed out that it is well understood throughout the acquisition community that the chief determination of system performance and cost occurs at this program stage. Investing a little more time and money in the program's early phases would yield the highest returns in design efficiency.

The majority of the teams expressed reasonable comfort with the program's schedule even though it clearly required significant concurrency, in the form of advance funding of subsequent phases to obtain supplier bids and complete early tasks. One contractor team singled out the program's schedule as problematic, stating that insufficient time was provided in Phase I for team formation. This contractor believed Phase II would not allow enough time for preliminary and contract design of the Arsenal Ship—that is, generating tradeoff studies and presenting those results to the potential user community for feedback. In addition, some said the schedule required long-lead investments before a Phase III award.

All contractor teams indicated that they would have participated in Phase I even if the program plan had called for a single winner for Phase II. None of the teams thought that provision of life cycle cost estimates in mid-Phase II had a significant impact on their Phase I concept design.

## Phase II

As anticipated by both the contractors and the ASJPO, the three teams awarded Phase II agreements substantially matched the $15 million government funding. By midway through Phase II, some ASJPO members believed that Phase III funding was "very aggressive," while others simply stated that it was underfunded by at least the previously reported figure of $100 million. In spite of this, the ASJPO stated its belief that the critical risk reduction task of systems integration would be about 80 percent complete in the demonstrator.

During this phase, the ASJPO stated that the shortness of Phase I was now causing difficulties. As a result of the schedule constraint, the ASJPO described the contractors as not pushing technological innovation as much as they might have. By the middle of Phase II, the contractors recognized the impact of Phase I's brevity, stating that it should have been about a year in length. As a result of Phase I's length, Phase II was now too short to evolve their designs sufficiently for them to propose the "best" design solution for Phase III. One contractor team noted that the length of, and government funding for, Phase II were insufficient to facilitate the hard engineering required to make the CAIV process truly effective.

## UNIT SAILAWAY PRICE

### Phase I

In general, the contractor teams proclaimed their belief that the USP goal of $450 million was both achievable and affordable. Several projected a USP well under the goal in their Phase II proposals, leaving significant room to account for the cost growth that occurs in most major weapon-system acquisition programs. Others projected a cost at or near the goal USP, stating that they could achieve it provided they kept ownership of the system specifications. No team proposed a USP higher than the $450 million goal. The teams apparently saw the USP not-to-exceed threshold of $550 million as irrelevant because the program would become unaffordable at that price.

At the time our interviews following Phase I ended, the contractor teams expressed varying levels of uncertainty with their USP estimates. The more confident tended to provide the ASJPO more detail in their Phase II proposals. There also seemed to be varying opinions as to how prepared the ASJPO was to assess the cost information it was provided.

### Phase II

The ASJPO cited one critical flaw in the CAIV process the contractor teams used in Phase II: their method of allocating the USP among the various components of their designs. The allocations were primarily based on how well each functional area could justify its estimate. This created an allocation that gave those areas with the best understanding (and therefore the lowest risk) the funds they requested, while allocating those areas with the poorest understanding (and therefore the highest risk) funds that were left over.

Generally, the hull, mechanical, and electrical were the best understood areas regarding cost. These structures and systems were mostly Off-the-Shelf (OTS) or modified OTS. The contractors' VLS system, which was a new design in all three cases but was based on an analogous system and could therefore be reasonably estimated, was the next-best understood. The least understood were the Command, Control, Communications, Computers, and Intelligence (C⁴I) and combat systems. The best analogous systems to these had their design, development, and production managed by the Navy, making their cost estimation extremely difficult for the contractors. The program office believed that the imbalance in allocation of the cost goal would degrade performance if a better scheme were not adopted.

The USP took a back seat in the minds of the contractors during Phase II, as the challenge of designing and building the demonstrator within the Phase III budget consumed them. A final USP figure was not provided to the government due to the program's cancellation, but in general the contractors still felt that the production Arsenal Ships could be built under the threshold price, if not for the goal of $450 million. A more detailed understanding of their own designs led to higher USP estimates, and one contractor in particular found its USP submitted at the conclusion of Phase I to be grossly underestimated. This contractor was well on its way to a proposed design concept with a credible USP within the threshold at the time the program was canceled.

A secondary source of cost growth in the USP estimates cited by the contractor teams at the end of Phase II was that of NRE efforts in Phase V. The funding in Phase III was considered so inadequate that major NRE efforts that were initially envisioned for Phase III by both the contractors and program office were deferred to Phase V. They hoped to recoup the cost of these activities by allocating them to the production ships, thus significantly increasing the USP.

## CONTRACTOR TEAMING AND BUSINESS ARRANGEMENTS

### Phase I

Some contractor teams formed quickly. Other contractors used existing consortia from another program as a foundation for their Arsenal Ship team. One team had no formal agreements, using simple collaborative agreements with their partners, and verbal assurances within their corporate structure. Some lead firms indicated a willingness to make changes to their team's membership in future program phases if they believed it would improve the program's chances. Most of the contractor teams planned or expected their arrangements to formalize in later phases of the program, with the possible establishment of a joint venture or limited liability corporation for Phase III and beyond.

Some teams reported no preferential accounting treatment, while others went as far as treating Phase I activities as an externally funded Individual Research and Development (IR&D) effort. Some teams used a "virtual corporation" business arrangement. Most teams reduced overhead by avoiding or minimizing applied General and Accounting (G&A), Facilities Capital Cost of Money (FCCOM), and fee. Flatter management structures enhanced decision authority and accountability.

New independent business units, independent cost centers, and the continued use of the "virtual corporation" were envisioned for future program phases. The teams organized to exploit the talents of their members as well as internal corporate divisions of the lead firm while avoiding overhead expenses. In all cases, the goal was the same: reduce total costs through a reduction in applied overhead and overall low capitalization while providing a distinct organizational unit with clear decisionmaking authority for the program.

### Phase II

The ASJPO reported that the teams' composition, coupled with recent industry mergers and nontraditional business arrangements, contributed to the innovative design of the Arsenal Ship concepts taking form by the middle of Phase II. The ASJPO further stated that the high quality of team interactions strongly contributed to what they considered a relatively successful program at that time, the middle of Phase II. They added that recent industry mergers allowed new technologies to be brought in and applied to various subsystems that were part of the design.

The ASJPO described the IPPTs from the various contractor teams as shaped by corporate cultures and roles within each contractor team. The prime contractor of each team dominated the IPPTs to varying degrees. One contractor team suffered from internal management struggles throughout Phase II; this team adopted a new and significantly different work allocation at the beginning of the phase. The team members seemed to be rather guarded, perceiving each other as potential competitors. The best explanation the program office offered for this team's difficulties was the overlap of core competencies among its members. The other teams had markedly better company-to-company relationships.

The ASJPO noted that there were no innovative business practices initiated in Phase II beyond those implemented in Phase I. Some subcontracting and other external relationships were different, changed to take advantage of the lack of requirement flow-down the traditional process involved. The prime contractor in each of the three teams was a traditional defense contractor; thus, its whole structure was organized around compliance with government business practices. The contractor teams reported that obtaining financial relief from most of the overhead built into government business processes would require separating the Arsenal Ship program from the parent organization.

Early in Phase II, some of the contractors envisioned this separation for Phase III and beyond, but the motivation to incur the one-time costs of creating such an organization quickly evaporated when the program was reoriented toward the SC 21 in April 1997. Most teams felt the reorientation reduced the probability of Phase V to nearly zero. With the amount of corporate investment in Phases I and II, the challenge to break even in Phase III, and the vanishing profit incentive of Phase V, the decisionmakers at these companies abandoned investing in a new business entity to execute the balance of the program.

## INTERACTIONS BETWEEN THE CONTRACTOR TEAMS, ASJPO, AND OTHER GOVERNMENT OFFICES

From the beginning of the program, the contractor teams generally treated DARPA as the customer for Phases I and II, and felt that the Navy would be the customer for subsequent phases.

### Phase I

During Phase I, the ASJPO provided minimal additional guidance beyond what was in the formal program documentation regarding system characteristics. The objective was to get industry to develop new concepts. The office wanted to facilitate whatever directions the contractors took in their system designs, not to direct the contractor's efforts. ASJPO's technical role was limited to simply understanding the concepts. This approach restrained technical exchanges between the contractors and the program office, with the intent to maximize industry innovation without government influence.

Program office responsibilities included answering questions about the CONOPS and SCD, providing access to government information, maintaining regular communication with industry, and conducting periodic program reviews. The ASJPO's role was characterized as "supportive without being directive—industry makes decisions."[3] The program office's description of its role during Phase I was to "provide and gain insight into the Industry team's activities, not to provide oversight."[4] The ASJPO facilitated access to publicly available information if the contractor was having difficulty obtaining it, but the contractor was responsible for identifying useful information and for any costs associated with gaining access to it.

The teams had disparate experiences and opinions regarding their interactions with the ASJPO. Some felt interaction was hindered by the small staff size, while others did not perceive a difficulty. Those contractor teams who realized the ASJPO's role was more reactive than proactive seemed comfortable with it. The contractors who did

---

[3]Arsenal Ship briefing, 7 May 1996, Dr. David Whelan.

[4]Arsenal Ship Program Rules of Engagement.

not adjust to this arrangement had trouble recognizing their need to initiate interactions.

The ASJPO felt that no particular management style had been adopted in Phase I, but noted that the transfer of responsibility changed the roles of the program office and contractors. The dissatisfaction indicated by some contractor teams might have been a result of their difficulty in adjusting to this unusual government-industry relationship. The ASJPO reported that these contractors often wanted the government to provide design decisions.

Some contractors felt that the ASJPO was weak in two functional areas during Phase I: cost analysis and $C^4I$. They indicated that increased staffing might have alleviated these weaknesses. The ASJPO noted that senior Navy laboratory and headquarters staffs, with extensive experience, provided cost analysis expertise. The ASJPO also stated that their $C^4I$ billet was not filled as quickly as they would have liked. The ASJPO emphasized that cost analysis was a critical factor in the Phase II down-select process.

The contractor teams generally gave the ASJPO high marks for keeping the schedule and meeting all of the milestones. Some of the teams indicated dissatisfaction with the specialist briefings given early in Phase I, stating that these presentations had marginal value. Most of the contractors experienced some difficulty in interacting with Navy organizations during Phase I, particularly the Naval Surface Warfare Center (NSWC) labs.[5] They felt that the ASJPO could have improved these interactions.

The use of IPPTs was new to some contractors. Although the contractor teams used IPPTs in Phase I, no ASJPO representatives were on these teams. All contractor teams thought that the IPPT approach was useful, and that future government participation on their IPPTs would similarly be beneficial. At the conclusion of Phase I, the contractors generally expected and wanted the program office's participation on IPPTs as a team member in future phases, but not in a directing role. In Phase I, the ASJPO utilized IPPTs with members from

---

[5]NSWC labs are the Carderock, Crane, Dahlgren, Indian Head, and Port Hueneme divisions of NSWC.

government organizations including NAVSEA, ONR, and the NSWC labs.

At the end of Phase I, some worried about IPPTs that would include both government and contractor members during Phase II. The primary concerns were the continued competition among the three remaining contractors, the protection of each contractor's proprietary information, and the availability of government personnel to participate on IPPTs, given the small size of the ASJPO. An additional concern was the extent to which government participation on contractor IPPTs could substitute for more traditional review and oversight procedures. The contractors wee concerned about getting feedback from the government on their performance in meeting the goals of Phase II.

## Phase II

The ASJPO took a much more active role in Phase II, working with the contractors on their demonstrator and production functional design concepts. The ASJPO became part of the contractors' top-level IPPTs. Its purpose was to react to problematic design aspects, rather than suggest what the design aspects should be. The ASJPO saw its role as one of "review and advise," or "consult"—not one to approve, check, or guide. Some teams responded to their technical suggestions better than others. The technical meetings with the contractors went much smoother than in a traditional acquisition environment. The absence of change orders, letters, and legal claims expedited the evolution of the designs.

Members of the ASJPO noted that the mix of backgrounds and skills within the program office itself was not appropriate, considering the overall technical content and highest-risk areas. The program office had, in relative terms, too much expertise in shipbuilding—arguably the area with the least technical risk—and not enough expertise in software, information systems, and $C^4I$, the areas of highest risk. This was noted by the contractor team that, coincidentally, appeared to have the most advanced understanding and capability regarding these high-risk areas.

Members of the ASJPO said the contractor teams put together a better blend of the skills required to execute the program. This adjustment to the program office's imbalance was made possible by the contractors' ownership of the requirements and concept design. The ASJPO attempted to compensate for their shortcomings by spending $100,000 on an outside contractor. The consulting contractor commented on the contractor teams' software designs, and met with the teams to review their software development process.

Because three contractor teams participated in Phase II, some in the ASJPO felt that the IPPTs did not provide them with sufficient process insight. These individuals stated that the program office lacked the staff to participate on the lower-level IPPTs; as a result, they felt that they did not have enough exposure to the contractors' activities to truly understand how each was doing. Some expected this problem to haunt them at source-selection time.

The ASJPO expected that having only one contractor team in Phase III would allow it to gain adequate insight through reliance on the IPPTs. At the time of program termination, the program office was still in the process of defining its role for Phase III.

## OVERALL IMPRESSIONS

### Phase I

The contractor teams appeared to be satisfied with the program at the end of Phase I. The program structure and management approach generally were viewed positively, contributing to cost savings in various ways. DARPA's Section 845 OTA, along with the ASJPO's enlightened interpretation of DoD Directive 5000.1, allowed streamlined oversight and reporting, and gave the contractors design and cost control. The USP goal was believed achievable if the government allowed the contractor to retain complete design control. The contractor teams were in agreement regarding most program attributes.

### Phase II

The contractors liked the unique acquisition approach. By Phase II, they had adjusted to their enhanced role, and enjoyed it. The program office and contractors both described the approach as enabling innovation, allowing decisions to be based on common sense, and facilitating commercial business practices. The ASJPO described the contractors' work as outstanding.

Members of the ASJPO found themselves extraordinarily busy during Phase II, with high travel burdens. Some bemoaned their inability to engage in various tasks, as well as their lack of detailed knowledge of the contractors' designs.

Many on the contractor teams expressed their personal disappointment with the program's end and their impending return to the usual acquisition environment. They expressed disillusionment with the prospect of readjusting to the inefficient, bureaucratic, constrained, and confrontational business practices inherent in that environment. Many in the program office were similarly vexed with their impending return to the normal procedures of their parent organizations.

# Chapter Six

# PROGRAM ISSUES RESULTING FROM THE ACQUISITION PROCESS

We unearthed a number of issues directly resulting from the unique acquisition approach during our interviews with the contractor teams and ASJPO. Most concerned the contractor teams, but some affected the program office and others affected everyone. These issues are set apart from the general discussion on the acquisition approach because their causes, and the efforts to address them, merit special consideration. It is our hope that this discourse will assist future program offices using streamlined approaches to recognize potential problems and avoid them.

Only one of the issues listed below was fully resolved prior to the program's cancellation; at that point, most were only beginning. We list and discuss them in the approximate order in which they appeared.

- MK 41 VLS
- Interactions with the NSWC labs and Navy PARMs
- Following the "program of record"
- Lockheed Martin's proposed merger with Northrop Grumman
- Insufficient developmental funding
- Irrevocable USP offer and fixed price development
- Conversion of the demonstrator

## MK 41 VLS

Several Navy ship types requiring VLS capability currently use the MK 41 VLS. It is the only operational VLS that accommodates the array of ordnance expected to be used by the Arsenal Ship (as indicated in the SCD). Lockheed Martin is the sole-source developer, manufacturer, and provider of the MK 41 VLS for the Navy.[1] Early in Phase I, Lockheed Martin's Aerospace and Naval Systems division offered the system to all Arsenal Ship competitors, including the team led by Lockheed Martin's Government Electronic Systems division. The offer price was approximately $138 million per shipset (assuming 512 VLS cells per ship), which amounts to more than 30 percent of the Arsenal Ship's USP goal.

Several contractor teams found Lockheed Martin's offer insidious. The competing contractor teams pointed out that this price quote did not provide for the complete system; Lockheed Martin's Launch Control System (LCS) was excluded, which is the only LCS that is weapons-certified for use with the MK 41 VLS. Lockheed Martin would provide a price quote for the LCS once a contractor agreed to use the MK 41, effectively diminishing that contractor's control in their CAIV process for meeting the USP goal. The offer also did not include updated technical manuals for the MK 41 system; thus, this would also have to be negotiated separately. As a point of reference regarding the complete cost of the MK 41 VLS, the procurement and installation price in 1994 for a 64-cell system was $26.3M, which equals about $29M in FY98 dollars.[2] This comes to $232M for a 512-cell shipset—more than half the USP goal.

Only seven shipyards are currently qualified to install the MK 41 system, most of which work exclusively for the Navy. Any contractor team without one of these shipyards would be at a competitive disadvantage, due to the complex and peculiar nature of the MK-41 installation process. None of these shipyards is a leader in the commercial ship-building industry, which is the type of shipyard an

---

[1] Lockheed Martin letter offering the MK 41 to Arsenal Ship competitors dated 23 May 1996.

[2] *Navy/DARPA Arsenal Ship Program: Issues and Options for Congress,* CRS Report for Congress, 97-455 F, April 1997. We believe this price includes the LCS, but cannot be sure because our source did not mention it.

Arsenal Ship competitor might choose given the program's intent to exploit commercial industry techniques in order to keep within the USP constraints.

NAVSEA was slow in releasing MK 41 VLS detailed design drawings to the Arsenal Ship teams for potential inclusion in their designs. If the contractor team chose to develop its own LCS, weapons certification of that system would be required.

Thus, the contractors generally believed that the Lockheed Martin team had an unfair advantage. The teams felt that the ASJPO should have offered the MK 41 VLS, including its LCS, as GFE.

The ASJPO had a different view. The office responded that every team had unique experience and technologies that enhanced its competitiveness. Because a VLS was not mandated, each team conceivably could design one with less acquisition cost, lower installation costs, an open architecture for adaptation to future needs, and decreased maintenance and manpower costs. The ASJPO explained that the program specifically precluded GFE, and that the point of doing so was to give the contractors total design control. The contractor teams would be free to create design solutions that would be less costly to acquire and operate. The ASJPO noted that the high handling and processing fee charged by the Navy's GFE procedure, using PARMs, would be an additional cost.

The circumstances surrounding the offer of the MK 41, and the competing teams' general discomfort with turning over control of a third to a half of the weapon system's value to a company not on their team, led some of the teams to develop new VLS designs during Phase I. These contractors noted that Lockheed Martin's MK 41 VLS offer price was the current price to the government, which included all costs associated with the implementation of DoD Instruction 5000.2-R, as required for MDAPs. The price therefore included an inherent cost penalty when compared to a new system under the Arsenal Ship acquisition approach.

The issue was circumvented by the middle of Phase II. The remaining three teams, including that led by Lockheed Martin, developed new VLS designs. The ASJPO reported that all three new designs were improvements over the MK 41, good programs that would be less expensive. At the end of Phase I, however, the new VLSs were considered major risks. Hardware testing of some of the designs occurred during Phase II. Midway through Phase II, risks in all three designs had been considerably reduced.

In spite of the program's cancellation, some contractors are marketing their VLS concepts as a cost-effective alternative to the MK 41. If one of these new designs is ultimately developed, the government and contractor will benefit. As predicted by the ASJPO, a next-generation VLS would open up a new market for its producer, and motivate cost and performance improvements to the existing MK 41.

## INTERACTIONS WITH THE NSWC LABS AND NAVY PARMS

What the ASJPO was trying to accomplish in the Arsenal Ship program was fundamentally at odds with the business practices and incentives that are part of the Navy's traditional acquisition community. The contractor teams did not have the authority to compel the NSWC labs nor the Navy PARMs to provide them with information and access to data or equipment. DARPA officially managed the program through the first two phases; thus, the Navy was not in command. These circumstances provided disincentives to the Navy's functional offices to offer input and support. The ASJPO said that these organizations simply did not understand the Arsenal Ship program, and would not work outside their usual methods.

### NSWC Labs

Early in Phase I the contractor teams noted that each NSWC lab appeared to have its own policy on interacting with them. The ASJPO indicated that the program was primarily designed to leverage industry's technology, not that of the labs. For this reason, the ASJPO did not provide guidance for these interactions prior to Phase I. At the 7 May 96 Industry Briefing, one lab distributed a "brochure" listing technologies and services available for a fee. The ASJPO did not approve, stating that the lab "was premature in marketing its services within the Arsenal Ship context." The ASJPO considered lab involvement of this sort "as hindering industry's own thought process development."

To resolve the issue, the ASJPO clarified the role of the NSWC labs during Phase I through the signing of an MOA on 6 August 1996. The labs were permitted to negotiate Agreements directly with industry teams. They could provide nonexclusive products and services that would be limited to the use of test facilities and the provision of objective data. They were barred from providing advice or interpretations, and source-selection evaluators were specifically excluded from participation in services to industry. They could contract only services not available in the private sector.

In spite of this remedy, some of the contractors—particularly those with little experience with these organizations—remained confused about how to engage the NSWC organizations through the balance of Phase I. The ASJPO felt that the problem stemmed from the cultural change required as a result of the transfer of design responsibility to the contractors. Contractor teams that had prior dealings with NSWC labs were accustomed to having government-developed technologies handed to them that they were to incorporate into their system. Teams that had no history with these labs needed more time to understand what they offered; these could have benefited from advice by the ASJPO on how to access the lab's experience and expertise.

For Phase II, the ASJPO implemented a new MOA on 9 January 1997. It clarified the role that the NSWC labs would play in Phase II, which was greater than their Phase I role. The Phase-I MOA rules applied, with the added options of providing technical expertise in the form of consultation and recommendations or opinions. The MOA carried a large, nonexhaustive list of areas of technical expertise available to the industry teams. Explicitly stated in the Phase-II MOA, and conspicuously absent from the Phase I MOA, was a requirement for NSWC headquarters' concurrence in the labs' Agreements and funding arrangements with the contractor teams.

The labs' increased role in Phase II required them to accommodate the unique needs of each contractor team through individual Agreements. Each team required unique assistance from the labs because the contractors created their own system specification, and the lab work done for each team directly affected its design. In addition, the Phase II schedule constraints required the work to be done without delay. The labs had difficulty with these demands.[3]

The Phase II contractor teams had difficulty getting the labs to accommodate their schedule pressures. The model tests conducted for two of the teams by the NSWC Carderock division was a valuable contribution to those teams' efforts, but in some instances simply took too long. Additional difficulty occurred with structuring payments to the labs for support work. The contractors noted that working- and middle-level lab personnel were eager to help and excited about the new approach. However, the top levels of management appeared to drag their feet, treating the contractors' requests as low priority. The contractors stated that they had no leverage with the labs because the labs were not profit-making enterprises, and therefore had no real incentive to help the contractors succeed.

The ASJPO could not help the contractors out of these difficulties, primarily because the labs and ASJPO report through different lines of authority. In spite of these difficulties, the program office believed that two contractor teams made good use of the lab's capabilities during Phase II. The team that tried using a different source for these services had similar problems.

## Navy PARMs

A primary advantage of excluding GFE from the Arsenal Ship program was the resulting exclusion of the Navy's PARMs. PARMs manage the development and procurement of most major subsystems onboard Navy vessels. The subsystems are developed independently from the ships that ultimately use them. Each subsystem is developed in "stove pipe" fashion, and must be integrated onto the lead ship. A traditional major surface combatant depends greatly on the PARMs—the DDG-51 program office deals with approximately 58 PARMs.

---

[3]The traditional acquisition process calls for the labs to provide to all contractors what information the lab thinks is necessary. Because the traditional process requires all contractors to bid to the same detailed specification, any information released to one contractor is released to all, a process known as "leveling." This fosters a level playing field in the competition.

The goal of excluding GFE from the Arsenal Ship was to facilitate the contractor's complete control of the design of the weapon system. However, the inherent connectivity of the Arsenal Ship concept, and the use of existing weapons as defined in the SCD, in effect required that the Arsenal Ship be integrated with some existing systems.  In Phase II, the contractors minimized their dependence on PARMs. Only three existing systems, which were considered unavoidable, were used in their designs:  ATWCS, CEC, and Aegis.[4]

In theory, working with only a few PARMs should not create the lack of program control that program offices working with dozens of PARMs experienced.  The acquisition approach of the Arsenal Ship program means that the PARMs should treat the contractors as customers.  There was no mandate that the contractors use PARM-managed systems; thus, the PARMs should be motivated to please the contractors or risk their looking elsewhere for a specific capability. In practice, however, each PARM has a monopoly on its system's specific capability, and the contractor has nowhere else to turn.  The contractor might be able to reinvent the necessary capability, but often would lack the resources to do so.

Some described the PARMs as having difficulty accepting the program's business approach.  During Phase II, they were said to be reluctant to cooperate with the three Arsenal Ship contractor teams. One explanation provided for their reluctance was that they did not want to waste time with two of the teams, because only one would remain in Phase III.  The ASJPO freely admitted that it had failed to get full cooperation from the PARMs during Phase II.

To integrate the ATWCS, CEC, and Aegis systems properly with the Arsenal Ship during Phase III, the contractor team would need intimate knowledge of these subsystems' designs and access to the software that makes them function.  Changes in each subsystem's software would have to interface with the Arsenal Ship weapon system.

---

[4]ATWCS is the Advanced Tomahawk Weapons Control System, which is a current upgrade to the system necessary to fire the Tomahawk missile. It is one of the most important, if not the most important, weapons specified in the SCD. CEC is the cooperative engagement capability that is currently being integrated into weapon systems DoD-wide so that all weapon-firing platforms can share targeting data. Aegis is an integrated network of computers and displays linked to sensors and weapon systems able to simultaneously detect, track, and engage numerous air and surface targets.

This level of access to the PARMs' subsystems' software was unacceptable to them.

The PARMs were not accustomed to having to answer to a contractor. Profit was not a motive, and they were given no real incentive to work with the contractors. The efforts to transfer detailed data and integrate systems required by the contractors seem directly contrary to the PARMs' self-preservation motivation. Sharing their system with a contractor in the Arsenal Ship program might lead directly to competing with that contractor in the future. Specifically, any PARM who expected that the coming SC 21 program would require its system's capability might not want to create a competitor by cooperating with an Arsenal Ship contractor.

At the time of the program's cancellation, the extent of the PARM issue was just being realized. The ASJPO was trying to develop a business arrangement that was both acceptable to the PARMs and would give the winning Phase-III contractor the insight required to integrate properly the necessary subsystems into their design. The contractors feared that, even if an arrangement were agreed to, the PARMs might stonewall in order to be certain that the contractor failed to integrate appropriately the PARM-controlled subsystem, thus ensuring the need for the PARM itself.

## FOLLOWING THE "PROGRAM OF RECORD"

In Phase I, the ASJPO and contractor teams disagreed about whether the "program of record"—the funding and schedule for all program phases as outlined in the Phase I solicitation—would come to pass. The contractor teams stated that they wanted the program to unfold as planned, but were having a difficult time believing that the government would be able to stick to the plan. The ASJPO steadfastly asserted its commitment and ability to keep to the plan.

As early as the end of Phase I, most of the contractor teams indicated that if the program became more like traditional acquisition processes, such as requiring increased reporting or oversight, the program would exceed the planned schedule and funding. The contractor teams considered this a serious issue that would likely arise when the program transitioned from DARPA to Navy management, which they expected to occur before Phase III was completed. The ASJPO expected this transition to occur sometime during or shortly after Phase IV, well after the demonstrator's construction. The ASJPO also expected that all work on the demonstrator would be conducted under the Sec. 845 OTA, freeing the contractor team from the DoD Instruction 5000.2-R process and the feared changes in the management approach.

Another difficulty the contractors foresaw at the end of Phase I was the large increase in funding between FY97 and FY98 ($48 million to $188 million as of December 1996) required as the program moved from Phase II to Phase III. Programs are commonly subject to external scrutiny (Congressional Budget Office, Congressional Research Service, Genral Accounting Office) and to congressional budget cuts when funding dramatically increases. The realization of this possibility would make Phase III funding even more inadequate. At the end of Phase I, the ASJPO specifically stated that it did not anticipate difficulties with full funding for Phase III. When pressed on this issue, the ASJPO noted that the program's funding stream had been presented to Congress, the Navy's comptroller office, and the Office of the Secretary of Defense (OSD) comptroller office; none objected to the year-to-year funding profile.

Just three months into Phase II, the Navy changed the program and renamed it the MFSD. No official document of the change exists. The ASJPO was never officially notified. DARPA appears not to have officially recognized this Navy-initiated reorientation. This may be an important factor to explain why the ASJPO continued with the program of record. The Navy notification took the form of an announcement by Rear Adm. Murphy, the director of the surface warfare division in the office of the Chief of Naval Operations, the week of April 14–18 at a classified industry conference. Murphy stated that this change might answer congressional critics about the Arsenal Ship's requirements and concept.

The ASJPO formally notified the contractor teams that same week, but the form of its notification did not reflect the magnitude of the reorientation. The letter stated, "The Navy is planning on using the Arsenal Ship Demonstrator, in parallel with its primary tests to evaluate the military utility of the Arsenal Ship, to evaluate various SC 21 technologies." The letter went on to state that the "testing can be accommodated within current demonstrator designs." It then provided a list of SC 21 technologies envisioned to reduce risk via sea testing on the demonstrator. The ASJPO viewed the motivation behind the change as the need to justify research and development funding with greater return on investment. It felt that Arsenal Ship technologies demonstrated through the MFSD were intended to support not just the SC 21 program, but the CVX[5] as well.

At that time, the press described the change as follows: ". . .the Navy will merge the arsenal ship program into the more defined SC 21 'family' of ships."[6] This appears to have been the more accurate depiction. The change effectively merged the Arsenal Ship and SC 21 programs, and put a demonstrator-only emphasis (no production ships) on the Arsenal Ship program.[7] As a direct result, the contractor teams wanted to abandon the program of record.

By the middle of Phase II, Congress had expressed concern about the apparent disconnect between the two programs. In addition, Arsenal Ship production (Phase V) funding was not in the Navy Program Objective Memorandum (POM). When questioned about this shortly after the program's reorientation, Murphy stated that the Navy would not have to make a decision to buy successor ships until FY02, when the demonstration of the first prototype was complete. He went on to state that the first production Arsenal Ship would not be built until FY04.[8] This was a large breach in the program of record's schedule, which called for exercising the Phase V option in the third or fourth quarter of FY01.

The contractor teams faulted the program office for continuing with the program of record in light of these circumstances. They characterized the Navy-imposed reorientation as the beginning of the end of the program, and saw the ASJPO's commitment to the program of record as destructive. The contractor teams believed that the ASJPO should have abandoned it, reorienting the program toward supporting both the Arsenal Ship and SC 21 programs. They believed that,

---

[5]The CVX is the first aircraft carrier planned to follow the CVN 77.

[6]*Inside the Navy,* 21 April 1997.

[7]*Navy/DARPA Maritime Fire Support Demonstrator (Arsenal Ship) Program: Issues Arising From Its Termination,* CRS Report for Congress, 97-1044 F, 10 December 1997.

[8]*Inside the Navy,* 21 April 1997.

had the program been restructured shortly after the April reorientation, its status might have improved in the eyes of both the Navy community at large and Congress. A restructure may also have allowed the program to continue under the vastly reduced (compared to what the program of record called for) funding provided in FY98.

Midway through Phase II, the ASJPO acknowledged that program changes that the Pentagon and Congress made were their biggest difficulty. The office was aware that the contractor teams were concerned about the program's developments, and knew that the changes had affected the motivation and perception of the industry teams. In spite of this, the position of the ASJPO remained that the Arsenal Ship and SC 21 programs were separate, and that five production Arsenal Ships were planned. The program office either chose, or was directed by DARPA management, to virtually ignore the Navy's changes to the program. The ASJPO indicated that severe budget cuts might require modification of the program plan, but it planned no changes at that time.

## LOCKHEED MARTIN'S PROPOSED MERGER WITH NORTHROP GRUMMAN

The pending merger of Lockheed Martin and Northrop Grumman, announced on 3 July 1997, created differing opinions regarding effects to competition for Phase III, and the strategic behavior of the newly formed corporation. Shortly after the announcement, the ASJPO stated that it did not expect the merger to be finalized until after the Phase III down-select; thus, the two Lockheed Martin[9] teams would finish Phase II as separate entities. The ASJPO hoped the two firms would honorably complete their Phase II commitments independently.

Some ASJPO officials were skeptical, and suspected collusion. They noted that both Phase III proposals submitted by the Lockheed Martin teams could offer to add substantial corporate funding in Phase III, effectively "buying into" the program. This strategy would make it quite difficult to justify selecting the third contractor. At the

---

[9]The Northrop Grumman name was to be dropped entirely in the combined corporation's name.

time the program was terminated, the ASJPO was planning how to handle this scenario should it come to pass.

To the ASJPO, choosing one of the newly merged firm's designs for Phase III would create additional, previously unanticipated uncertainty. Should one of the Lockheed Martin designs be selected for Phase III, the lack of firm specifications in the program created the opportunity for the shipyard, or the ensuing design, to be changed. Barring specific language in the Agreement amendment for Phase III, Lockheed Martin could literally discard facets of its winning design while substituting those from its losing design. Should it win, the third contractor team would be far less likely to make such radical changes, since it would be working from its single design effort and from a single corporate teaming arrangement. At the time the program was canceled, the ASJPO was considering what language to use in the proposed Phase III Agreement to limit sufficiently the winning contractor's authority to change the design.

## INSUFFICIENT DEVELOPMENTAL FUNDING

Throughout the contractor teams' 18-month affiliation with the program, they viewed Phases I–III as seriously underfunded, but only viewed the underfunding of Phase III as a serious problem, labeling it the most serious issue in the program even before Phase II began. The competing teams seemed to agree that taking a loss on Phase III via the inclusion of corporate funding would be unacceptable. The general feeling was that the nonrecurring engineering and demonstrator construction costs were simply addressed inadequately in the available $389 million budget.

By the middle of Phase II, the contractors became convinced that Congress would not provide funding beyond the original $389 million specified for Phase III. As a result, the "real" trade space for their system concepts was severely constrained. They sped the removal of components and capabilities from their evolving demonstrator designs. Much of the systems integration and automation previously planned for the demonstrator was eliminated. This caused the crew sizes for the proposed demonstrators to be significantly larger than those envisioned for the production configuration. The redundancy needed to provide reliability was almost completely eliminated. The program office was in the loop, reluctantly accepting changes as the contractors degraded their designs.

Those in the program office agreed that these actions would seriously damage the adequacy of the demonstrator. One ASJPO member stated that, regardless of which contractor team won, it remained uncertain whether the demonstrator would have enough capability. A second member said the underfunding was forcing the contractors to compromise the design and thus hinder the demonstrator's ability to demonstrate the concept. A third member stated that the unrealistic cost goal of the demonstrator resulted in a demonstrator not configured like the production ships and not able to test the performance objectives fully.

The contractors agreed that production in Phase V was uncertain; thus, they might not recoup losses from Phase III during production. Several teams also believed that the funding for Phase III and the USP for Phase V were inconsistent. The Phase III funding-to-USP ratio (that in a traditional ship acquisition program is roughly equivalent to the ratio of a lead ship's cost to that of follow-on vessels) was far too low, given historical experience for Naval surface combatants. Some contractors feared that under the planned Phase III funding, the demonstrator would not be properly able to portray the full potential of the weapon system, thus jeopardizing the continuation of the program.

The contractors reported that, as Phase II progressed, the scope of the developmental tasks envisioned for Phase III grew. This was not because the desired capabilities for the system changed; rather, it resulted from incorrect assumptions made earlier in the program. The government described some capabilities and technologies during Phase I as off-the-shelf that were actually still under development. Some expected these technologies eventually to be off-the-shelf, but not in time to support the Arsenal Ship program schedule. The result was that the Arsenal Ship program would have to pay the previously unanticipated cost for the development of those technologies deemed necessary to the weapon system.

Many believed that the ASJPO should have engaged the contractor teams in an open dialog about what resources would be required in Phase III to ensure a successful demonstrator, and to develop a design concept that would optimize the weapon system's life-cycle cost. One team suggested that shifting funds from Phase V to Phase III would have provided a better system for the same total expenditure. An ASJPO official stated that the acquisition experiment embodied in the Arsenal Ship program would make sense only if the front end of the program were fully funded. Another program office member said that one of the program's lessons was that cost constraints imposed by the government needed to be based on a firm estimate with analytic support. The best solution the program office offered shortly before termination—given the constraints it faced from powers outside the program—was to relax the nonrecurring engineering and software development in Phase III by deferring these activities to Phase V.

## IRREVOCABLE OFFER AND FIXED PRICED DEVELOPMENT

### Irrevocable Offer

At the end of Phase I, all contractor teams expressed a willingness to provide, in their Phase III proposal, the required irrevocable offer to meet their self-determined USP. Some, however, thought there was little chance they would be required to stand by their offer, and that providing such an offer before completing the detailed design of the ship was not practical. The immaturity of their designs at the end of Phase II, coupled with the program's structure and the uniqueness of the vessel, fostered the belief that their offered USP would not survive to production in Phase V.

The contractors believed that the experience gained during Phases III and IV would almost certainly precipitate design changes that would render the offer irrelevant. In the process of building a demonstrator that was both producable and functional, the contractor team would likely need to change the design that was defined at the end of Phase II. These changes would result from the "unknown unknowns" that inevitably crop up when any complex system is built for the first time. If funding for Phase III became tight, which all parties agreed was likely, design changes would become even more likely. The Navy would likely identify capability deficiencies while operating the demonstrator in Phase IV as well, thus precipitating other design changes.

An additional objection to the USP irrevocable offer was that it amounted to fixing the production price prior to detailed development. The result removed the opportunity to recoup unanticipated development losses from Phase III while in production in Phase V. One of the contractor teams tried to mitigate this concern by estimating the deferred nonrecurring costs from Phase III and allocating them to the USP for the five production ships in Phase V. Accurately identifying and calculating these costs in advance is a formidable challenge.

The final concern with the irrevocable offer was the ambiguity about what form the contracting terms and conditions would take upon implementation. Some felt that defining these so that all parties would agree upon interpretation now and in the future was also a formidable challenge.

When pressed, all teams said at the end of Phase I that they would be able to meet their irrevocable offers if ultimately required to do so. The use of commercial shipbuilding practices and the freedom to make tradeoffs in system capabilities and specifications would enable them to meet their specified USP offer.

## Fixed Price Development

At the end of Phase II, one of the contractors stated that the program structure—including fixed funding in Phase III, the irrevocable offer for Phase V, and the technical matrix attached to the Phase III solicitation—amounted to fixed-price development. The matrix required the contractor to index the technical information for all elements of the design. The ASJPO requested a detailed accounting for the entire system, which amounted to a de facto design specification.

According to this contractor team, the performance matrix, as defined by the ASJPO, bound the performance for the Arsenal Ship and demonstrator. The contractor saw this as binding the system specification, and felt that this was requested too early in the development process. In addition, the contractor stated that when it questioned the ASJPO, the contractor realized that the program office did not understand how the matrix was to be understood, interpreted, and used. These demands and uncertainties alarmed the team's corporate directors, who reacted by adding terms and conditions (change clauses) to their proposed Phase III Agreement modifications. These clauses were intended to provide an escape out of the irrevocable offer. Similar thoughts must have occurred to all the contractor teams; the ASJPO noted that all teams added terms and conditions to this effect in their proposed Agreements.

All parties to the program knew that congressional action would be required for the OTA to apply to production, and for it to extend beyond December 1999. However, shortly after Phase II began, the Navy testified to Congress that the program would become an MDAP, subject to DoD Directive 5000.1, if production Arsenal Ships were produced.[10] This shows that the Navy did not intend to seek an extension of the OTA for Phase V; as a result, the irrevocable offer would ultimately be unenforceable.

The program office asserted that the approach was not fixed-price R&D as long as cost was not so constrained that the contractor team was prevented from making trades, such as reducing capabilities. The authors agree that, as long as the winning contractor was not held to the system specified in the technical matrix required in the modified Phase III Agreement, the approach would not amount to fixed-price development. If, however, the ASJPO held the contractors to the matrix, their characterization would appear correct. In any event, the meaning of the matrix was ambiguous enough to justify the contractor teams' alarm.

## CONVERSION OF THE DEMONSTRATOR

The program of record required the cost of converting the demonstrator as part of the contractor's Phase III proposals. In light of the change in the program to the MFSD, the ASJPO had the contractors submit two bids for the conversion scheduled for Phase V. The first asked them to schedule the conversion effort at the best time in their Phase V production plan, assuming the demonstrator would sustain normal wear and tear during its Phase-IV demonstration. The second required the conversion in a specific year to accommodate the

---

[10]Statement of John Douglass, Assistant Secretary of the Navy for Research, Development, and Acquisition, to the House of Representatives' Committee on National Security, Military Procurement Subcommittee, meeting jointly with Military Research and Development Subcommittee, 26 February 1997.

planned "reuse" of the vessel as a demonstrator for the SC 21 program.

As a direct result of the insufficient Phase-III funding and the degradation of the "completeness" of the demonstrator designs that evolved during Phase II, the demonstrator's planned conversion made little sense by the end of Phase II.  No matter which contractor won Phase III and built it, subsequent conversion to the production configuration would not be cost-effective.  The combination of its incompleteness and the absence of a price goal for conversion to the production configuration in Phase V led the contractors to disregard the cost of its conversion.  The demonstrator designs in development at the end of Phase II reflected this.  One of the designs was described as so costly to convert that the approach recommended by its builder was to cut off and "throw away" the front two-thirds of the ship.

Independently, the ASJPO said that the option to convert the demonstrator probably could not be exercised contractually.  The modification of the vessel in support of SC 21 was not defined; as a result, the state of the vessel when returned to the contractor for conversion was not determinable.  It follows that any calculations made in providing a price quote for the conversion would almost certainly be inconsistent with the condition of the demonstrator when it was through supporting both programs.

# Chapter Seven

# OBSERVATIONS AND CONCLUSIONS

Weak or nonexistent Navy (and therefore congressional) support determined the course of the program, buttressed by the gross underfunding for Phase III. Strong support might have rescued the funding. One might describe the results of the acquisition approach as cruelly ironic. The freedom it afforded within the program provided for great success *internally* in achieving the goals of its first two phases. However, the approach also created uncertainty and even hostility from the relevant *external* forces, namely, specific stakeholders in the Navy community and those with specific agendas in Congress.

In this chapter, we begin by describing the circumstances that led to the gross underfunding of the program of record's first three phases and an explanation as to why it went uncontested. Given the previous discussions that all but prove the contractors could not make a profit in the developmental phases of the program, we then describe the motivations that kept them in it. We follow this with an analysis of the program's cancellation and how the acquisition strategy might have contributed to it. Finally, we analyze which facets of the acquisition approach appeared to be successful, which were not, and the probable reasons for both.

## THE UNDERFUNDING TALE

### Underfunded from the Beginning[1]

The amount NAVSEA originally estimated for the demonstrator portion (Phases I–IV) of the Arsenal Ship program, using a traditional acquisition approach, was $600–700 million.  This estimate did not include the construction of an all-new vessel.  The estimate was supposed to cover primarily nonrecurring engineering tasks; some said it lacked rigorous analysis to support it.  The estimate was simply cut in half when the streamlined acquisition approach with a CAIV emphasis was envisioned.  The resources to execute the demonstrator portion of the program recommended to John Douglass, ASN (RDT&E), and Adm. Boorda, the Chief of Naval Operations, were $350 million plus a DDG-51 destroyer that would be converted to serve as the demonstrator ship.  Somehow, this recommendation was misunderstood.

A memo bearing Douglass's and Boorda's signatures was put out requesting a $350 million program, a figure the Navy later ratified at the program's inception.  The required DDG-51 was not mentioned in the memo.  This omission was probably an oversight by the staff members who drafted the memo.  In addition, it is possible that both Navy officials were led to believe that this funding was sufficient.  In any event, the absence of the required DDG-51 in the memo was ignored  because no one wanted to embarrass the high-level Navy officials.

The decision to let the contractors inform the government of the gross underfunding—which they never did—was itself made unofficially.  When Larry Lynn of DARPA saw the Navy's $350 million program-funding, and the absence of an existing Navy ship to use for demonstration, he knew that the funding was insufficient.  He secured as much DARPA funding as possible, $170 million, which was significantly more than DARPA had originally intended to contribute.

---

[1]The events described in this section are a direct account given by an ASJPO official who was involved in the described activities from start to finish. The official gave the account in the presence of several ASJPO members and members of this study team. The authors have no documented proof of the alleged activities, but found no evidence contrary to the account, nor reason or motive for its falsification. Therefore, we find the account credible and include it here.

## Why No One Made an Issue of It

Phase III funding was insufficient to create a representative demonstrator. By the conclusion of Phase I, both the contractors and the ASJPO knew that. The issue was raised by the Source Selection Advisory Board during the Phase II down-select process, but went unresolved. The problem was avoided during Phase II even though both sides saw it worsening as they became more knowledgeable about the technical challenges embodied in designing and building the demonstrator. The time for rationalizing the cost of development was during Phase II, before expectations for a $389-million Phase-III price became so entrenched that divergence would be perceived as failure.

Throughout the first two phases of the program, the contractors refrained from openly acknowledging the development-funding shortfall because of the competition. Their tactic appeared to be to win Phase III, eliminating the competition; then they would petition the ASJPO to adjust funding to ensure construction of a successful demonstrator.

Two factors kept the ASJPO silent about the insufficient funding. The first was its commitment to accomplishing Phases I–IV for the specified $520M, i.e., executing the "program of record." More importantly, the tepid (at best) support for the program in Congress and by the Navy kept it silent. The ASJPO must have believed that acknowledgment that the program would need additional funding would precipitate its cancellation. The office apparently felt that the only "hope" the program had was for the attitude of these external powers, particularly the Navy, to change before the need for additional Phase III funding became acute.

The growth of both cost and schedule in the prototype design and manufacturing phase of the Global Hawk program predicted what would most likely have occurred in Phase III of the Arsenal Ship program. By the end of Phase I of the Arsenal Ship program, nonrecurring funding had been added to the Global Hawk program. The reorientation of the Arsenal Ship program toward supporting both the Arsenal Ship and SC/DD 21 that occurred early in Phase II provided a perfect opportunity to deviate from the program of record. This event arguably could have been characterized as expanding the program's scope, justifying additional funding in Phase III.

## Why the Contractors Continued with the Program

The Agreements signed by the contractors at the beginning of Phase I, and modified for the winners of Phase II, allowed for either the contractor team or the government to stop work at any time, given a specified notification period. In a traditional contractual arrangement, only the government retains this right. The contractor teams sustained losses in Phases I and II, and suspected that they would be lucky to break even in Phase III. The ASJPO planned for more traditional language in the Phase III agreement that would exclude the contractor's ability to exit the program (but not the government's), require cost sharing of overruns, and include a limitation-of-funds clause. Why were the contractors continuing under this acquisition approach?

From the program's beginning, the contractor teams had a variety of reasons for their participation. All stated that they would have participated even without the innovative acquisition strategy. Many considered the program important both to evolving the acquisition strategy and developing technologies for the future. Reasons cited for participating included development of technical knowledge, process knowledge and experience, and lessons regarding teaming. The participating corporate divisions used these reasons to persuade their headquarter organizations to invest the funds the early stages required. As with any program, the potential for profit also motivated participation.

Throughout the program, both the contractors and the program office stated that one important motivation, if not the most important, for the contractors' investment and participation in the program was the resulting improvement in competitiveness for future system acquisitions. All parties specifically mentioned the SC/DD 21. When the Arsenal Ship program was reoriented toward the DD 21 in April 1997, this motivation appeared to be paying off. As the prospect for Phase V declined, and the profits from building production ships became less likely, the DD 21 motivation became even more important in keeping the contractors from exiting the program. Some of the contractors, specifically the ship builders, were thoroughly discouraged by the decreased probability of production Arsenal Ships. Their commitment to the program faded during Phase II.

This motivation—competitive advantage in future business—is not unique to the Arsenal Ship program. It applies wherever a relatively small program leads to opportunity in a coming larger program, regardless of acquisition approach. The streamlined acquisition approach used in this program is relevant because it magnified the motivation. The contractors not only positioned themselves well for the SC/DD 21, but also gained experience in streamlined processes that might well be the wave of the future. This could boost the contractor's competitiveness in future business opportunities.

## INADEQUATE NAVY SUPPORT EQUALS NO PROGRAM

Absent explicit support by the chief executive or an organized congressional lobby, congressional support for any acquisition program is shaped by the procuring service's resolve to move the program forward. When a user service is behind a particular program, it will give that program the time and energy, at all levels, to make it as successful as possible in the eyes of Congress and the public. The service undertakes a parallel effort to convince Congress of how essential the program is to national security. The service educates and shapes the thought processes of congressional advisors as well, using a combination of hard work and skilled marketing.

The user-service mainstream never supported the Arsenal Ship concept, and therefore program. The most basic reasons were that they either did not believe it would be helpful (e.g. for Marines onshore calling for fire support), or they believed that it would replace traditional platforms (e.g. Navy carriers and strike aircraft, Air Force strike aircraft). These beliefs shaped the behavior of high-level Navy officials and members of Congress, which in turn affected the behavior of Navy organizations, the ASJPO, and the contractor teams.

While only the authors assert that a program truly desired by the military is "marketed" to Congress and to those who shape the debate influencing its survival, we are not alone in our belief that the Navy's tepid support for this program was the chief cause of its cancellation. DARPA specifically stated that the program was canceled as a result of a lack of funding in FY98, which was a direct result of "the Navy's poorly articulated and ambiguous legislative strategy for the Demonstrator."[2] The authors assert that, had the Navy truly wanted the program, its legislative strategy would have been clear.

The following is a discussion of the reasons behind the lack of advocacy by the Navy and other services. Where appropriate, we distinguish between how the Arsenal Ship concept and its program acquisition strategy contributed to the behaviors of the relevant parties.

## The Loss of Admiral Boorda

The Arsenal Ship program was understood to be the brainchild of Adm. Jerry M. Boorda. From the beginning, the program's very nature went against the grain of the Navy's acquisition organizational infrastructure. Without Adm. Boorda, the program probably would never have existed. His death in May 1996, just two months after the program's inception, meant the program no longer had a champion.

Had Adm. Boorda issued a rudimentary Mission Need Statement to underpin the program's CONOPS and SCD, the Navy would have found it difficult to waver in its support of the Arsenal Ship concept in his absence. The program's acquisition approach is directly responsible for the absence of such a document. Those who preside over future streamlined programs should take note of the importance of having such a document to ensure that the military utility of the weapon system concept has been established.

Without its powerful and influential advocate, no one remained to sell the concept and program acquisition approach to Congress and the Navy community. This fact was not lost on the contractors; in our interviews conducted at the end of Phase I (December 1996), they specifically noted that the program needed such an advocate— politically—if it was to proceed past Phase II.

---

[2]DARPA's 30 October 1997 letter to the program's three contractor teams in which the Phase III solicitation was canceled.

## The Threat to Force Structure

The CINCs generally welcomed the Arsenal Ship when it was portrayed as an addition to the Navy's force structure. However, the successful fielding of the proposed six-ship fleet was seen as possibly providing justification for replacing or reducing the number of other Navy (and possibly Air Force) force structure elements. The Arsenal Ships could undermine both services' long-term agendas to minimize the shrinking of their force structures. As a direct result, this would undermine the established carrier and strike user-based constituencies as well.

If the Arsenal Ship succeeded in its missions, a change in the calculus for determining the size of U.S. forces required to fight and win two major theater wars almost certainly would occur. The number of aircraft-carrier groups deemed necessary to support the national defense strategy might be significantly reduced; the number of long-range bombers, tactical fighter wings, and associated support forces thought necessary in the Air Force might likewise be reduced.

These potential results undermined support for the Arsenal Ship at the highest levels of the Navy and Air Force. This threat to force structure was a direct result of the unique system concept.

## The Threat to the Navy's Acquisition Corps

The Navy's existing acquisition community would be in jeopardy if the program's unique approach produced reductions in cost and schedule, as well as accelerating technological innovation. Many services provided by the acquisition corps within NAVSEA might no longer be needed. The Arsenal Ship acquisition approach was structured specifically to exclude the Navy's ship-design power centers from the process.

This threat largely explains the difficulties the program office and contractors had in their relations with the NSWC labs and Navy PARMs. The program was structured to adopt an approach directly counter to, and in fact specifically designed to circumvent, the notorious conservatism of the senescent Navy ship-building community. Some of the contractor teams reported that some NSWC labs felt threatened by the program's reliance on industry.

## The Funding Threat to the SC/DD 21 Program

Regardless of congressional predisposition for or against the Arsenal Ship concept, most within the Navy and Congress would characterize the program as an addition to the Navy's planned modernization strategy. In the current budget environment, the program would almost certainly compete for funding in what could be described as a zero sum game—that is, any funding for the program would only take funds from some other Navy program.

In the near term, the program most likely to compete with the Arsenal Ship for development funding is the SC/DD 21, the other Navy surface combatant program to be developed within the Five Year Defense Plan (FYDP). Both the Arsenal Ship and SC/DD 21 concepts would require hundreds of millions of dollars in development funding in the fiscal years 1998–2003.[3] If both ship types were built, they would be built concurrently, with the first production version of each most likely requested in the FY04 budget.[4]

This perspective appears rather myopic if one takes a broader view on affordability. The total expected funding for the development and production of six Arsenal Ships is relatively small when compared to other Navy surface combatant programs. The total acquisition was expected to cost $3–4 billion,[5] with funding spread over twelve years. The initial cost estimate for development alone of the DD-21 is $1.94 billion.[6] A striking comparison is the cost of a single Nimitz-class

---

[3]Almost $500 million for the Arsenal Ship program and about $750 million for the SC/DD 21 program, according to the statement of Rep. Curt Weldon (PA), given on 26 February 1997 in joint committee hearings. The initial DD-21 Selected Acquisition Report, dated June 1998, shows funding of more than $1 billion (BY1996) for the DD 21 during these fiscal years.

[4]Section 2.4 "Phase V Alternative Profile" of the final *Arsenal Ship Program Phase III Downselect Solicitation* (MDA972-97-R-0003) shows the initial production Arsenal Ship funded in FY04. This is the only production schedule shown in the solicitation. The initial DD-21 Selected Acquisition Report, dated June 1998, shows funding for the lead ship of the DD 21 class in FY04.

[5]See Appendix C for a detailed cost comparison of the Arsenal Ship to other Navy ship programs.

[6]Taken from the initial DD-21 Selected Acquisition Report, dated 30 June 1998. The SAR figures are adjusted from $1.86 billion BY96 to $1.94 billion BY98 to be consistent with the BY98 figures for the Arsenal Ship.

aircraft carrier, which is $5–6 billion and is typically funded in a single fiscal year.

In the year between the Arsenal Ship program's inception and the Navy's announcement reorienting the demonstrator toward supporting both programs, the Navy's analysis of the two programs was aimed at bringing them together. By February 1997, the Navy had incorporated the Arsenal Ship into their Cost and Operational Effectiveness Analysis (COEA), now known as the AOA, for the SC/DD 21. The Navy's FY98 budget request did not include "out year" funding for production Arsenal Ships. The Navy apparently saw that building both ship types would be unaffordable.

In the six months between the program reorientation announcement and the cancellation of the program, the SC/DD 21 concept took on characteristics envisioned for the Arsenal Ship, including low observability and a small crew size. In a budget environment that made the Navy feel that they must select between the two programs, their choice was an obvious one. Many in the Navy saw the Arsenal Ship as a mere stepping stone to the SC/DD 21, which one might characterize as the "favored son" of the surface combatant acquisition community. All agree that the SC 21 is a more versatile platform that plays a prominent role in the Navy's long-term vision of its force structure.

## CONGRESSIONAL AGENDAS

Two facets made the Arsenal Ship's acquisition more political than other weapons systems acquisition programs. The weapon system concept represented a new class of ships, the first new class since the ballistic missile submarine in the early 1960s. As a result, it threatened the existing allocation, or balance, of mission assignments. Most new weapon systems are built directly to replace an aging predecessor; these do not "tread on anyone else's turf" because the mission for the new systems is the same as for the old. The primary mission of the Arsenal Ship was one that no single existing system could perform: support a land campaign with hundreds of long-range weapons that could be fired almost immediately. Weapon systems in inventory today that contribute toward accomplishing that mission, primarily aircraft carriers and long-range bombers, have constituent bases that would like to see their systems perpetuated and not displaced by the Arsenal Ship.

The second politicizing facet in the Arsenal Ship program was the aforementioned threat to the Navy's acquisition infrastructure. This community is usually pleased with a new system acquisition because such an endeavor requires its expertise. The Arsenal Ship program required only limited and specific expertise from the Navy labs and PARMs, and only because they held a monopoly on those services or systems.

As a direct result of these two facets, three constituent bases had specific reason to be unenthusiastic about the program: manufacturers of competing weapon systems; host facilities for competing weapon systems; and the large traditional Navy acquisition infrastructure. In all three, large numbers of jobs are at stake in specific states (senators) and Congressional districts (representatives). The industrial interests that build, and in some cases maintain, weapon systems that would have ultimately competed with the Arsenal Ship for its mission had good reason to motivate their representatives against the program. Congressional members that represent districts in which these systems and others are stationed or home-ported are also concerned about preservation of jobs.

A primary example is Newport News Shipbuilding, which is the largest private employer in Virginia and the only shipyard in the U.S. capable of building Nimitz-class aircraft carriers. If the Arsenal Ship brought enough firepower early on to a theater of war, the need for the current fleet of a dozen aircraft carriers might very well be questioned. As a result, production of new aircraft carriers might not be supported as older ones are retired.

Northrop Grumman is another example. There is significant overlap in the missions envisioned for the B-2 bomber and the Arsenal Ship. This corporation would prefer an order valued at roughly $15 billion for 20 more B-2 bombers, rather than compete for a $2.5–3 billion order for five Arsenal Ships and the conversion of the demonstrator.

The congressional B-2 lobby, with the agenda of procuring additional aircraft and composed of members with large numbers of B-2 related jobs in their districts, does not want another weapon system competing for the B-2's mission. The power of specific committee and subcommittee assignments played prominently in the Arsenal Ship's fate. Two ardent B-2 supporters from the Military Procurement Subcommittee—the chairman, a representative from California (where much of the bomber's development and production takes place), and the ranking member, a representative from Missouri (where the current B-2 bomber force is stationed)—worked to undermine the program.

An unfortunate by-product of the streamlined acquisition approach used in the Arsenal Ship program was that it provided the program's enemies in Congress with reason to question it. The oversight and reporting customarily provided by the MDAP process was conspicuously absent in the acquisition process. The approach removed most top-level oversight and requirements. There were no Defense Acquisition Board (DAB) milestones or documents, no MNS, and no COEA or AOA. This created genuine grounds for skepticism at the congressional level. Some members used the lack of oversight as reason, rightly or wrongly, not to support the Arsenal Ship program.

## ACQUISITION APPROACH IMPLICATIONS

We intend the following insights to be applicable to both traditional program acquisition approaches and streamlined ones such as that for the Arsenal Ship. The presumption is that transfer of these insights to the broader acquisition community will improve acquisition program management processes and outcomes.

An innovative acquisition strategy similar to that used in the Arsenal Ship program should be implemented as a package. While the key elements of the strategy are distinct and identifiable, they interact with each other in a complex fashion. The elements of the acquisition strategy—minimal weapon system specification, contractor design responsibility, small joint program office, affordability constraints, integrated product and process teams, Section 845 OTA—are mutually enabling and reinforcing if properly executed.

In future implementations of this acquisition approach, a few provisions will facilitate execution of the strategy. All except the last were present in the program:

- A program office staffed with high-quality, highly motivated government and private-industry personnel who believe process reforms are required.

- Elevating acquisition-process change to a program priority, thus ensuring that adequate attention is given to innovative strategies.

- A high degree of flexibility and proactivity in key program individuals. This includes a willingness by government and contractor personnel to take advantage of opportunities.

- Contractor commitment to taking full responsibility for outcomes. One must be willing and able to define realistic tradeoffs, and act on them in a manner that may be contrary to government preferences.

- Government commitment, at all levels and by all "stakeholders" (the greater Navy community and Congress), to the acquisition strategy and weapon-system concept. Support must be consistent and stable both politically and financially.

The following sections describe the successes, failures, and undetermined results related to the aspects of the Arsenal Ship acquisition approach. Failures resulted largely from poor implementation of the approach, not from a fundamental flaw.

The program's early cancellation made it impossible to assess the acquisition strategy in the context of the full range of acquisition tasks and phases. The adequacy of the acquisition strategy in the detailed design and production phases, and in the absence of competition, was not demonstrated. We draw conclusions only where we believe that enough transpired for them to be appropriate.

## Program Structure

The program structure fundamentally changed the relationships between the program office, supporting government organizations, and industry. As a result, government organizations outside the program office could be expected to have difficulty adjusting to a new way of doing business. Key players should jointly develop mechanisms for addressing program-office interactions with technical support organizations and facilitating direct contractor interactions at the outset.

The program showed that users (warfighting organizations) could be brought into the acquisition process early in a program's life cycle through a series of modeling, simulation, and subsystem exercises involving the contractors. This interaction appeared to improve user understanding of the designs, concepts, and available technology. The contractors' understanding of the user's preferences also improved.

The program demonstrated that reducing ship-acquisition cycle time for early program phases could be accomplished. The government's commitment to meeting stated milestones enabled a positive relationship with industry. However, evidence from other programs as well as projections from those involved in this program, suggests that if schedules are not determined using a firm analytic basis, then accelerating the initial phases of a program increases the risk of significant problems in later phases. In this program, the length and value of Phase II did not allow for enough hard engineering to make the CAIV approach truly effective.

One of the more radical characteristics of the program plan was construction of a demonstrator before making a production commitment. The value, in terms of risk reduction, of its construction to support early testing was not determined. An undesirable by-product of the program structure was the planned production gap between the demonstrator and production ships, which could be problematic because of the lack of continuity. In the years between the construction of a demonstrator and the first production version, most of what was learned during the former is forgotten. Also, those involved with the former are lost to other projects during the gap, and reassembling them will be partially successful at best. This effect is endemic to the ACTD and similar acquisition approach structures that attempt to demonstrate rudimentary operational capability before making a production commitment.

## Weapon System Specification

The use of two brief documents, the SCD and CONOPS, in lieu of traditional detailed specifications with firm technical requirements, appeared to be a success. This minimal specification facilitated the transferring of design responsibility to the contractors. It resulted in management flexibility that facilitated the proposal of innovative designs, and demonstrated the application of commercial practices and products to military systems.

The program office never felt that it had lost control of the program, or that the contractors deviated from the government's expectations for the weapon system. The lack of a firm system specification allowed the contractor teams and the ASJPO to interact in a way that actually improved the understanding of both parties during the competitive program phases.

## Contractor Design Responsibility

The contractor teams took responsibility and proposed designs that apparently would have met the government's desired operational capabilities. Contractor design responsibility increased the contractor's ability to make cost-performance trades and design changes, as well as incorporate design innovations. As one would expect, the government lost input in determining the design and capabilities of the system. However, this loss facilitated the significant development, production, and operating-cost reductions expected by all.

Serious problems remained in enabling complete contractor design responsibility. Those areas where the contractor teams had to rely on Navy organizations, especially for capabilities peculiar to the NSWC labs and utilization of legacy systems controlled by PARMs, were the most problematic. The incentives and behaviors of these organizations must change before their capabilities and talents, and those of their industry teammates, can be fully used. This can only be accomplished by changing the current organizational and command structure, putting the program offices at the top with these organizations subordinate. At the same time, this reorganization must facilitate Navy subsystem configuration control and the need for the Navy to maintain its capability as a "smart buyer."

## Small Joint Program Office

A small joint program office can effectively manage a streamlined program in its initial phases. The office's ability to draw on external expertise (e.g., labs), especially for source-election activities, enable it to function. To an extent, its success is tied to the level of design and management responsibility assumed by the contractors—the more the contractors take, the less staff the program office will require.

The DARPA-led program management had mixed outcomes. It provided the organizational context and culture necessary to implement an innovation acquisition strategy, but it hindered support from traditional mainstream service-acquisition and technical-support organizations. In future programs, this drawback might be mitigated by utilizing a partnership arrangement between DARPA and the Navy, and securing buy-in from these mainstream organizations concurrent with program initiation.

## Affordability Constraints

An inherently complex and challenging new weapon system apparently can be built within funding constraints, providing a sound analytic process determines the constraints. Contractors will make cost-performance trades in their designs if the government insists that cost caps be met. The USP constraint provides a mechanism for maintaining cost control and implementing CAIV.

However, because of the program's cancellation, we do not know how the affordability constraints would have played out. Using the USP process as a way to implement CAIV and maintain cost control was not fully demonstrated. The government did not demonstrate willingness to accept less performance and resist requirements creep. Preventing requirements creep and maintaining cost control in a sole-source environment may have been challenging in Phase III and beyond.

There was a clear mismatch between the Arsenal Ship's USP target and funding for the demonstrator. The latter would not have been sufficient to complete the nonrecurring engineering required in Phase III so that the production configuration envisioned for Phase V would be producable within the USP goal.  The unrealistically low Phase III funding severely limited the "real" trade space for the competing contractors.

In addition, the irrevocable USP offer at the end of Phase II was ill-conceived.  In an accelerated program of this type, the USP and nonrecurring engineering effort estimates are based on incomplete information.  The commitment to a production price before detailed design and development is a poor strategy that forces both industry and the government to make commitments before they are ready.

We cannot say that the USP threshold and crew size desired for the Arsenal Ship were achievable, but all parties thought them to be.  The nonrecurring funding for the first four program phases was clearly in error.  This resulted from mistakes made by the government prior to the program's establishment.  These mistakes crippled the program, but did not cause its cancellation.  Had the program continued, these errors would have, at a minimum, made the program appear to fail because of virtually unavoidable cost overruns, and might have precipitated its eventual cancellation because of perceived failure.

## Integrated Product and Process Teams

IPPTs with members from companies comprising individual contractor teams, those with members from government organizations assisting the ASJPO, and those with members including both government and contractor organizations, generally succeeded.  The intra-contractor teams' IPPTs enabled innovation and integration in the designs they offered.  The intra-government IPPTs greatly improved the government's ability during the source-selection process.  These IPPTs facilitated assessment of competing designs, and assessment of each contractor team's CAIV process.  In IPPTs with contractor and government representatives, contractor ownership of the weapon system design, and government inclusion on contractor IPPTs, provided a structure for improved government-industry interactions.  These IPPTs permitted government insight into contractor activities, and provided information in a more timely and less intrusive way than in a traditional oversight process.

Because of the program's cancellation, IPPTs were not tested in an environment without competition.  In Phase III and beyond, the use of IPPTs might have been even more successful because of the lack of competitive pressures and resulting removal of constraints on assisting and informing each other. On the other hand, and as seen in other programs, the lack of competition might have created an environment in which the government would attempt to dominate the decision-making process of the IPPTs, thus usurping the contractor's design control and CAIV process.

## Section 845 OTA

In implementing the OTA, context and perception may be more important to executing the strategy than specific waivers. Changing the mindset of government and industry personnel to enable confidence in creating innovative procedures is critical to successful implementation. The Arsenal Ship program largely achieved this. The OTA gave the freedom to practice "common sense acquisition." The program showed that the government-industry relationship does not have to be adversarial, even during competitive phases.

The use of Agreements provided a more flexible and manageable environment than traditional contracts. This included both the program's technical content and the ability to make changes without a formal approval process. The Agreements made possible the contractor's use of IR&D funding as a way to leverage the government's funding. The long-term implications of contractor investment of R&D funds, especially IR&D, to support the program, were controversial. The issue here is one of the most efficient and beneficial allocations of corporate R&D.

Freeing parties from compliance with DoD Instruction 5000.2, which effectively removed traditional oversight and reporting burdens, was generally a success. This freedom encouraged nontraditional firms to compete, but since none survived past Phase I, the goal of opening the program to nontraditional suppliers was only nominally attained. All parties felt that reducing government auditing and using contractor processes and reporting formats cut costs and cycle times.

The "insight" gained from the approach, as opposed to what is gained using "oversight" procedures, appeared to succeed. However, the optimum balance between "insight" and "oversight" with the absence of competition could not be determined because of the program's cancellation prior to Phase III. The program office effectively handled variations in processes and reporting formats among contractors. The key to successful use of the contractors' processes and formats was their clear and consistent application.

# GENESIS OF THE ARSENAL SHIP CONCEPT AND PROCESS

The Arsenal Ship weapon system presents an innovative operational concept for delivering large numbers of precision munitions from sea-based systems to support littoral warfare, theater air defense, and land battle. It also presents an innovative concept for achieving this mission. These conceptual innovations help explain the the origins of the Arsenal Ship program and process.

The *mission* concept is derived from studies regarding how the Navy can contribute more to the conduct of land-based warfighting capabilities, especially in providing artillery-like fire support[1] to lightly armored Army and Marine forces. This is consistent with the Defense Science Board (DSB) Summer Study, "Tactics and Technology for 21st Century Military Superiority," published in October 1996; the Army's long-term vision as outlined in "Army After Next"; and the Marine Corps' philosophical commitment to innovative change as embodied in "Sea Dragon."

The ideas underlying the *system* concept for the Arsenal Ship are founded in several sources. The first was an internal Navy concept for a "missile barge" that was considered in the spring of 1995. This ONR study looked at a concept with 1000 VLS, but did not address combat systems. A second study, conducted by the NSWC's lab at Dahlgren, looked at the feasibility of the combat systems during the summer of 1995. In spite of the latter study's relevance to the Arsenal Ship program, it was not shared with the contractor teams for fear

---

[1]The SCD states that the ship is to have space, weight, and support-system capacity reservations for future installation of an extended-range gun system.

that it might limit their vision of the potential solution space for the weapon system.

## Acquisition Process Motivation

The government is primarily motivated by system affordability and the recent Cost as an Independent Variable (CAIV) initiative, and has therefore adopted an acquisition process similar to that of the Tier II+ High Altitude Endurance Unmanned Air Vehicle (HAE UAV) program. This approach is consistent with a recent DSB report.[2] The acquisition process and affordability constraints are designed to motivate each individual industry team, which has complete control of its system concept, to leverage ideas and technologies from their unique set of military and commercial business experiences. In addition, industry looked toward the Smart Ship Program, MARITECH, and the Technology Reinvestment Project (TRP) for ideas on how to provide a design solution within the planned program funding.

The Smart Ship Project was initiated as a result of a Naval Research Advisory Committee's (NRAC) panel on Reduced Manning. The goal of the Smart Ship program is to reduce crew size and workload through the implementation of mature technologies, as well as changes in policies and procedures. The Aegis-class cruiser USS *Yorktown* (CG-48) has been designated as the initial demonstration platform. Ideas for crew reduction cover the full range of ship operations. Some significant reduction in crew size has already been demonstrated.[3]

To reduce operations and support costs, a core goal defined for the Arsenal Ship system concept is a minimal crew size (maximum of 50). While reduced manning on the *Yorktown* has been accomplished by applying technologies to legacy systems[4] and breaks with traditional Naval billeting practices, the Arsenal Ship would achieve

---

[2]DSB "Defense Acquisition Reform (Phase III)—A Streamlined Approach to Weapon Systems Research, Development, and Acquisition," May 1996.

[3]Of the initial 375 person crew, more than 90 had been eliminated as of early calendar year 1997.

[4]Legacy systems are those already in use by the Navy as part of one or more weapon systems.

its low complement through systems automation, utilization of capabilities indigenous to other fleet assets, and a low maintenance design emphasis for the hull as well as shipboard systems. Lessons from the Smart Ship Program may be applied to Arsenal Ship by facilitating systems design.

The MARITECH program, also managed through DARPA, is primarily intended to improve the commercial competitiveness of U.S. shipyards through the development and implementation of innovative technologies and manufacturing processes. The program is specifically intended to develop competitive, state-of-the-art designs and products that can be marketed internationally; and, to encourage improved, integrated design and construction processes to catch up with competition overseas and take advantage of the projected worldwide market expansion in ship construction. The program is expected to benefit the Navy through reduced ship-building costs via productivity improvements and reduced overhead.[5] The program solicitation suggests that the bidders organize as vertically integrated consortia or teams of shipyards, ship owners/operators, marine equipment suppliers, and ship and shipbuilding process technologists. Many of the cornerstones of the MARITECH program may well be leveraged in the Arsenal Ship's technology application and management concepts.

The Technology Reinvestment Project (TRP), established in 1993 and managed by DARPA, was intended to facilitate development of "militarily useful commercially viable technology in order to improve the DoD's access to affordable, advanced technology."[6] The TRP funded almost $700 million spread over 131 projects through 1995. All of the military services and several other government agencies participated. The program aims to leverage commercial technology developments through cost-share arrangements with industry. TRP activities that may benefit the Arsenal Ship involve innovative design and construction processes, repair and maintenance approaches, and propulsion concepts. Projects in the $C^4I$ and electronics manu-

---

[5]MARITECH Program description, DARPA (www.darpa.mil/asto/maritech. html).

[6]Fact Sheet: The Technology Reinvestment Project, DARPA (www.jdupo.darpa.mil/jdupo/info/trp_fact.html). TRP no longer exists in its original form. The remaining activities are managed out of DARPA's Joint Dual-Use Program Office.

facturing and packaging are also relevant to the Arsenal Ship. The TRP was considered an "investment partnership" and was therefore managed outside the traditional FAR-based acquisition process, thus potentially contributing to innovative system concepts for the Arsenal Ship, as well as providing an example of management outside of traditional acquisition processes.

# DESIGN ASPECTS OF THE ARSENAL SHIP WEAPON SYSTEM

Accomplishing the mission at the lowest possible life cycle cost drives the design characteristics of the Arsenal Ship concept. To perform its mission, the Arsenal Ship must possess the following characteristics:

- sustained forward presence
- passive self-defense
- joint connectivity
- automated engineering, damage, ship, and weapon control systems.

The following are details of these characteristics and the design aspects suggested to accomplish them as stated in the SCD and CONOPS.

## Sustained Forward Presence

The Arsenal Ship concept might be described as an addition to the U.S. maritime pre-positioning force. It would remain on station in support of a Unified CINC for an indefinite period, without dependence on a host nation's support or permission. The Arsenal Ship concept is similar to a Navy nuclear ballistic missile submarine in that it is deployed to an operational area where it awaits orders to launch ordnance.

The planned fleet of six Arsenal Ships was to provide "continuous availability" in three forward theaters. For six ships to provide this level of theater coverage, each vessel would be forward deployed for the majority of its operational life. The program plan requires achievement of a 2:1 ratio of inventory ships to war-ready, on-station vessels. This ratio is extremely low in comparison to other Navy combat ships that are on-station in a distant operation area.[1] If the Navy envisioned a ratio between 4:1 to 7:1, a fleet of 12–21 ships would be required to cover the designated forward theaters. Theater coverage with six ships can save billions in production and operating and support costs in comparison to a fleet of 12 or more ships.

The competitive market of the commercial shipping industry has created a great incentive for building ships that are highly reliable and need little time undergoing pier-side maintenance. Commercial hull designs, construction techniques, and applied treatments are engineered to minimize corrosion. The mechanical, hydraulic, electrical and other ship systems are built to be durable and easily maintained.

In contrast, commercial market or customer pressures have not affected Naval ship design and construction techniques. While reliability has always been a high priority for Navy vessels, Naval techniques have fallen behind the state of the art in creating more maintainable vessels.[2] The government's request for the use of commercial practices and components in the Arsenal Ship's design and construction sought weapon-system affordability throughout its life-cycle. Systems requiring little maintenance at sea enable affordability in operating and support, as do infrequent planned availabilities.[3] These characteristics support the six-ship forward deployment plan, as well as facilitate the small crew size envisioned for the system.

---

[1] *Navy/DARPA Arsenal Ship Program: Issues and Options for Congress*, CRS Report for Congress, 97-455 F, April 1997.

[2] Comments of the Arsenal Ship Life Cycle Cost Study Team, Summer 1996.

[3] An "availability" is the rough equivalent of a major depot maintenance action. The ship is removed from service for a period of months for major maintenance work. The system cannot be easily or quickly returned to service during this time should a contingency develop.

## Passive Self-Defense

The Arsenal Ship was conceived to be highly survivable in the entire littoral environment. Its budget constraints meant that its survivability depended upon passive self-defense capabilities.

Threats to the Arsenal Ship would have come from subsurface, surface, and airborne aggressors. The Arsenal Ship's passive survivability would need to be designed-in. Signature control and countermeasures could have made the ship difficult to detect, target, and hit. The ship had to be designed to provide the most protection possible for the VLS cells in case of a hit, and be difficult to sink. Mass tonnage and a multiple-hull design were envisioned as likely strategies to help keep a damaged Arsenal Ship afloat. For the ship to resist further damage after being hit, it would have to have been inherently stable in a damaged condition, incorporate damage and fire-fighting systems, and include redundancy in its critical operational and mission systems.

As with other surface combatants, the combination of the Arsenal Ship concept's characteristics presented a significant technical and acquisition-management challenge. Some of these characteristics are incorporated on certain types of subsurface, surface-combatant, or commercial vessels, but no ship type has all of them. Multiple hull designs are now required for new-build commercial tankers. Surface combatants generally incorporate countermeasures, stability in a damaged condition, fire-fighting and damage-control systems, and redundancy in critical operational and mission systems, but not with a small crew size. Submarine designs commonly have signature management, but not so surface combatants; the technology exists, but it has been selectively applied at full scale only sparingly. Signature management is one of two areas in the program that required technology push.

## Joint Connectivity

The joint-connectivity architecture embodied in this weapon system concept was motivated by two realities: the evolving doctrine that requires U.S. forces to fight as a single cohesive unit, and budget constraints requiring that the Arsenal Ship be acquired and operated at the lowest possible cost.

The "remote control" features of the Arsenal Ship concept were unprecedented for a sea-going vessel. Regularly deployed Aegis combatants would initially operate the ship; it would be able to respond to multiple commanders from multiple services to support multiple missions simultaneously. The "remote magazine" launch concept would have been made possible through employment of the Cooperative Engagement Capability (CEC), or a CEC-like system. Planned capabilities included remote missile selection, on-board missile initialization and remote launch orders, joint connectivity, and remote "missile away" messages to the control platform. No existing Navy vessel possesses these attributes to the extent envisioned for the Arsenal Ship, posing a significant technical integration challenge.

By leveraging the capabilities resident on Aegis combatants and other theater assets, the resources required for targeting, mission planning, and command/decision functions would not have been needed onboard the Arsenal Ship. Removing those capabilities would have directly reduced the design, integration, and production costs.[4] Likewise, the absence of these requirements would have eliminated the billets to perform these activities, to maintain the systems required for their execution, and the associated shore support infrastructure for personnel and equipment.[5] These would have reduced operating and support costs for the life of the system.

## Automated Engineering, Damage, Ship, and Weapon Control Systems

The goal of crewing the Arsenal Ship with no more than 50 mandated the automation of key shipboard systems, consequently reducing operation and support costs in comparison to other sizable Naval surface combatants. Such a small complement for a ship of the size, complexity, and military warfighting capability of the Arsenal Ship was a revolutionary concept. This is the second area in the program that required technological push.

---

[4]It should be noted that this approach might have increased the complexity and cost of integrating the Arsenal Ship with other warfighting systems, but much of that cost might already be embodied in the development of systems such as CEC.

[5]Billets might have had to be added to other ships to perform these functions.

Daily activities required to keep the ship battle-ready partially determine crew sizes on naval vessels, but so do the Navy's cultural and traditional practices. On existing ships, billet requirements can be dramatically reduced by revisions to the commanding officer's watchbill, and changes in the way the commander mans for Condition III (wartime steaming) and Condition I (general quarters). Eighty percent (40 billets) of the crew reductions demonstrated by the Smart Ship program in 1996–1997 were a result of these changes in practices.[6]

Some of the world's largest commercial ships have very small crews. There is no lack of proven technology and know-how for these vessels; the crew size of dry cargo ships, tankers, and bulk carriers is often two dozen or fewer persons. The automation of their key shipboard systems makes this possible. Commercial automation architectures were to be applied to those systems aboard the Arsenal Ship that are common to Navy and commercial vessels. The ship concept's automation architectures for C[4]I and combat systems, however, would be unique.

The systems aboard the Arsenal Ship would have been considerably more complex than those on the average commercial vessel; thus, their automation would have been technically challenging. The Smart Ship program would have helped meet these challenges. An integrated bridge system, damage control system, integrated condition assessment system, and standard monitoring and control system, all tied together with a local area network, have been integrated into the Smart Ship program's demonstrator, the USS *Yorktown*. This group of automated systems is only a fraction of those that were anticipated for the Arsenal Ship.

---

[6]Statement of Bob Bost, U.S. Naval Sea Systems Command at the Smart Ship Project: Reducing Shipboard Workload training session at the 30th Annual DoD Cost Analysis Symposium, 13 February 1997.

# SCHEDULE AND COST COMPARISON

To understand the expected cost avoidance and abbreviated schedule motivations behind the innovative and nontraditional acquisition procedures applied in the Arsenal Ship program, we have developed a historical database on the experience of comparable programs using more traditional approaches. While we recognize that the uniqueness of the Arsenal Ship concept means that there are no direct antecedents, aspects of traditional Navy ship-building programs will provide some basis for comparison. We compare development schedule duration and unit-production costs of programs using more traditional Navy acquisition approaches to the plan for the Arsenal Ship program.

We considered including a comparison to commercial-ship acquisitions, but determined that the combined differences in process and technical characteristics between military and commercial vessels are too great for a relevant comparison.[1] Regarding Naval vessels, we

---

[1]Regarding development process differences, products are mostly off-the-shelf in the commercial ship-building industry, and foster minimal development activity. Most commercial ship types require customers to choose between products much as consumers choose between various manufacturers and models for a new automobile; customers can specify options, but have little say in the basic design. An exception is cruise ship construction, in which the buyer can specify layout characteristics of the ship to some extent.

Regarding the production phase of the acquisition process, some commercial practices are applicable to the Arsenal Ship program, and will be addressed where appropriate.

Regarding technical differences in both development and production, Naval surface combatants such as the Arsenal Ship are far more complex than maritime vessels. Most of the sophisticated, highly technical, and expensive systems on Naval ships are

we have specifically excluded aircraft carriers, submarines, and small ships (boats), as we believe they do not provide meaningful comparisons.[2]

## COMPARATIVE SYSTEMS

We compare the ship-building programs of Navy acquisitions during the years 1980–1993 to the Arsenal Ship program. This constitutes the baseline for Navy acquisition procedures up to the significant acquisition reform efforts begun in the 1990s. Program information, and cost and schedule data used in our comparisons are taken from December 1996 and prior Selected Acquisition Reports (SARs).

The SARs are the best source of consistent program data over time and weapon systems. However, using SARs for our comparisons has several drawbacks. Official schedule data in the SARs usually begins with Milestone 1. Information regarding pre-Milestone 1 activity is sometimes included in the program history narrative but is often not available. Regarding program costs, some early development costs do not appear in SARs. Cost-tracking usually begins in the ship program's SAR when the program is officially established, thus excluding the cost of research that is accomplished by internal Navy organizations before a formal program exists.[3]

The basic characteristics of the Arsenal Ship and our comparison systems are shown in Table C.1. The programs that began in the early 1980s provide actual cost and schedule data for lead-ship development and production, and early follow-on production ships. Figures in the more recently begun programs are strictly projections. The top-to-bottom ordering of the programs in Table C.1 is significant. With the exception of the Arsenal Ship, the programs are

---

not needed on commercial vessels. Development, production, and integration of these systems drive the cost and schedule for a surface combatant.

[2]ACAT1 acquisition programs for small ship that were excluded: Advanced Amphibious Assault Vehicle (AAAV); LCAC/Landing Craft Air Cushion; MCM 1 Mine Countermeasures; MHC 51 Coastal Minehunter.

[3]Much the same could be said about Air Force aircraft, missile, and munitions programs. Weapon-system developmental research is conducted by Air Force Material Command at Wright-Patterson AFB and Eglin AFB, through the Aeronautical Systems Center and Armament Directorates, respectively.

**Table C.1**

**Comparative Systems—Program Characteristics**

| Ship | Program MS 1 | Quantity | Size (Long-tons) | Length | Beam | Accommo-dations |
|---|---|---|---|---|---|---|
| Arsenal Ship | N/A | 6 | 20,000– 30,000 L/T | 600'– 800' | 60'– 100' | 0-50 |
| T-AO 187 Oiler | 1980 | 16 | 40,000 L/T | 677'5" | 97'5" | 137 |
| Strategic Sealift | 1992 | 19 | N/A | N/A | N/A | N/A |
| AOE 6 Support | 1982 | 4 | 49,000 L/T | 753'8" | 107' | 667 |
| LPD 17 Amphibious Transport | 1993 | 12 | N/A | N/A | N/A | 720 Troops |
| DDG 51 Destroyer | 1980 | 57 | 8,300 L/T | 466' | 59' | 341 |
| LHD 1 Amphibious Assault | 1981 | 7 | 40,000 L/T[a] | 840' | 106' | 1873 Troops |

[a]Fully loaded.

listed in descending order from the lowest unit production cost per vessel to the highest. As one would expect, the vessels in the upper part of the table are relatively simple, while those below them are more complex.

The T-AO 187 Class Fleet Oiler operates as a unit of an underway replenishment group, or independently to furnish petroleum production to operating forces at sea. It is a low-technology vessel that requires virtually no development and employs few complex systems.

The Strategic Sealift vessel is a more recent ship-building program that began after the Gulf War. The program plans to acquire ships for afloat prepositioning of equipment and transportation of Army and USMC surge equipment from CONUS to contingency areas. The first five vessels will be conversions of existing ships. The remaining 14 will be new builds.

The AOE 6 Class Fast Combat Support Ship is designed to provide underway replenishment for the carrier battle group. The ship will carry munitions, petroleum products, and provisions. It will provide deliveries and receive fleet freight, mail, and personnel to and from combatant forces underway.

The LPD 17 Class Amphibious Transport Dock Ship will conduct the primary amphibious warfare mission by providing for the embarking, transporting, and landing elements of a Marine landing force in an assault by helicopters, landing craft, and amphibious vehicles.

The DDG 51 Destroyer is a multimission guided missile destroyer designed to operate offensively and defensively in an environment including air, surface, and subsurface threats. This surface combatant incorporates low-observability characteristics and the AEGIS weapon system as part of its integrated combat system. The ship supports air-dominance, maritime-dominance, and land-attack missions.

The LHD-1 Amphibious Assault Ship's primary mission is to embark, deploy, and land elements of USMC landing forces in an assault by helicopters and amphibious landing craft. The ship also serves as a sea-control and power-projection asset. The ship's capabilities include combat systems, medical spaces, chemical/biological/radiological defense, and handling aviation ordnance and landing craft.

Of the six comparison ships, the first three comprise the auxiliary category, and the second three are combatants.[4] In choosing those ship types most comparable to the Arsenal Ship, the three combatants are preferred to the auxiliaries. In analyzing the characteristics of the combatants, the Arsenal Ship would seem to be somewhat more complex than the LPD 17, and somewhat less complex than the DDG 51 and LHD 1. Due to the subjectivity involved in comparing the relative complexity of the three combat ships to that of the Arsenal Ship, all three are considered.

---

[4] "Jane's Fighting Ships 1985–86," p. 659.

## DEVELOPMENT THROUGH LEAD SHIP CONSTRUCTION SCHEDULE COMPARISON

At lead-ship contract award (Milestone 2) in the traditional Navy approach, and at the beginning of Phase III in the Arsenal Ship program, a contract or agreement was to be in place with a single contractor team. Both approaches call for the development and production of the first example of the new vessel. The demonstrator was to be close enough to the production configuration that it could be modified to that configuration. Its technical maturity was to be close to that of a lead ship.

One of the key goals of the Arsenal Ship program was to field an operational demonstrator for evaluation by theater CINCs in as short a time as possible. The reduced schedule time to acquire a demonstrator rather than a lead ship was one of the key justifications for the acquisition process adopted for the program.

For the Arsenal Ship and comparative programs, Figure C.1 shows the timeline for Milestone 1 through the onset of testing the lead ship.[5] Milestone 1 in traditional ship programs is defined as the completion of the type's Preliminary Design. We chose the elapsed time between these two events because it represents the time frame in which most development takes place. Phases II and III of the program were planned for less than four years. All of the comparison programs were either planned for or accomplished between five and ten years; the three auxiliary ships required between 5 1/2 and 9 1/2 years, while the three combatants required between 8 and 10 years.

Comparison of the Arsenal Ship plan to those of the other surface combatants shows a planned reduction in development time of 50 percent or more. Given the state of the program at its cancellation, we cannot determine if it would have achieved its planned schedule.

---

[5]In the Arsenal Ship program, the equivalent of Milestone I was the beginning of Phase II, and the planned delivery of the demonstrator at the end of Phase III was used as a proxy for lead-ship-in-the-water.

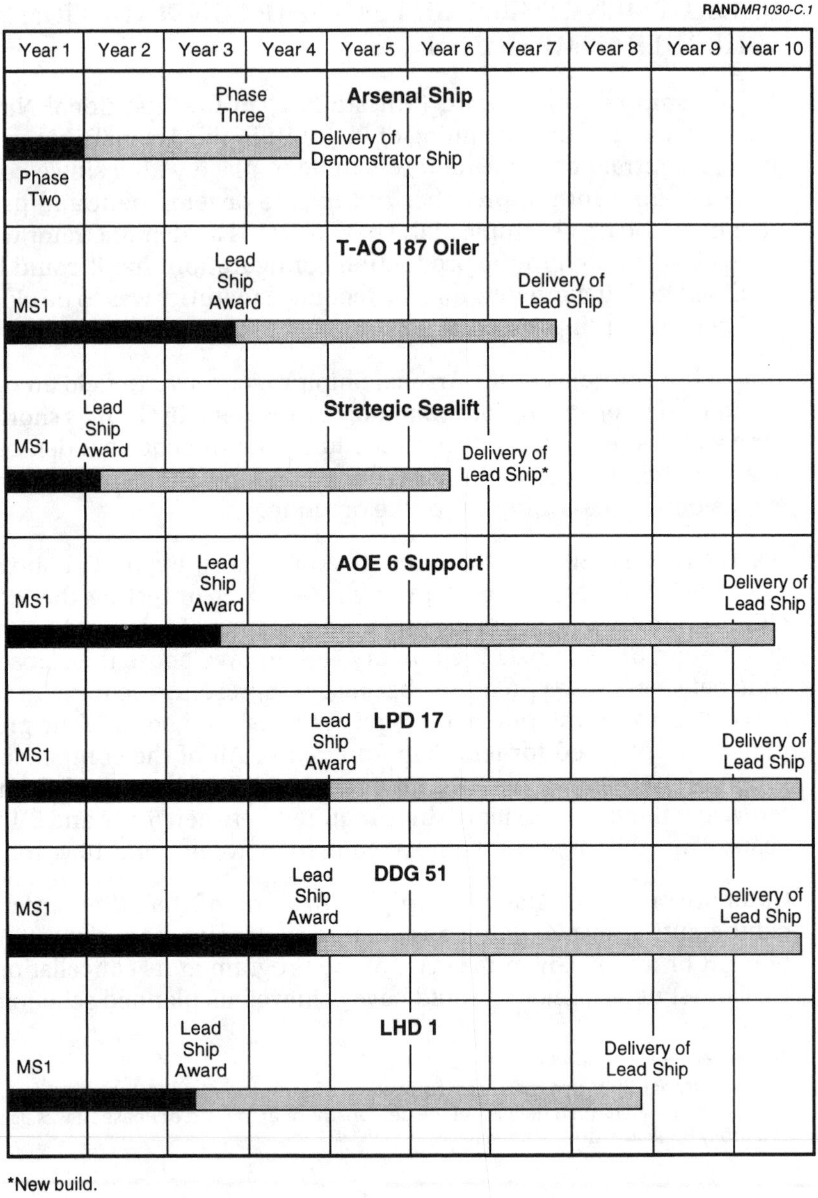

RAND*MR1030-C.1*

| | Year 1 | Year 2 | Year 3 | Year 4 | Year 5 | Year 6 | Year 7 | Year 8 | Year 9 | Year 10 |
|---|---|---|---|---|---|---|---|---|---|---|

**Arsenal Ship**
Phase Three
Delivery of Demonstrator Ship
Phase Two

**T-AO 187 Oiler**
Lead Ship Award
MS1
Delivery of Lead Ship

**Strategic Sealift**
Lead Ship Award
MS1
Delivery of Lead Ship*

**AOE 6 Support**
Lead Ship Award
MS1
Delivery of Lead Ship

**LPD 17**
Lead Ship Award
MS1
Delivery of Lead Ship

**DDG 51**
Lead Ship Award
MS1
Delivery of Lead Ship

**LHD 1**
Lead Ship Award
MS1
Delivery of Lead Ship

*New build.

Figure C.1—Comparative Naval Program Schedules

We also cannot determine whether schedule slip would have enabled the fielding of a sufficiently mature demonstrator to evaluate the concept's capability in an operational environment.

## SHIP CONSTRUCTION COST COMPARISON

Planned and actual costs for the Arsenal Ship and six comparative programs, converted to base-year 1998 dollars, are shown in Table C.2. The comparative systems' costs are from their SARs; Arsenal Ship cost estimates are as of January 1997.[6] The table shows total program funding, which includes government expenses and payments to contractors. We do not adjust for contractor profits, positive or negative.[7] As a result, corporate profits or losses on each program must be considered to show the true "cost" of each system from a resources-expended standpoint. The SARs do not provide the detail in cost information that was available for the Arsenal Ship program; thus, program cost estimates for the latter were aggregated roughly to conform to SAR data content definitions.

### Development Activities and Costs

Although ship programs usually have an R&D funding stream, it does not provide most of the funding for their development. There are two primary reasons for this. First, many ship and combat systems are provided as GFE to the prime contractor. GFE development activities are usually funded separately by the PARMs; thus, these costs do not appear as part of the ship's R&D funding (the DDG 51's AEGIS combat system is an exception). Also, nonrecurring system integration funding—an increasingly large portion of developmental activities and costs as ships become platforms for multiple complex electronics weapons systems—is buried in the procurement funding for the lead ship, and therefore is also excluded from the R&D funding stream.

---

[6]The Arsenal Ship cost estimate for Development Funding is taken from Table 2.2 - Arsenal Ship Program Obligation Plan circa January 1997. It includes the added funding in FY97 for a third Phase II contractor.

[7]Negative profits take the form of cost sharing, which all contractors elected for both Phases I and II.

**Table C.2**

**Comparative Systems —Program Costs**
**(millions of BY98$s)**

| Program | Development Funding | Average Unit Procurement Cost | Production Funding | Mil Con Funding | Total Funding |
|---|---|---|---|---|---|
| Arsenal Ship | $66 | $600[a] | $3,600[b] | N/A | $3,666 |
| T-AO 187 Oiler | $23 | $240 | $3,848 | N/A | $3,871 |
| Strategic Sealift | $43 | $301[c] | $5,719 | N/A | $5,762 |
| AOE 6 Support | $44 | $684 | $2,734 | $93 | $2,871 |
| LPD 17 Amphibious Transport | $91 | $772 | $9,267 | N/A | $9,358 |
| DDG 51 Destroyer | $2,905 | $937 | $53,437 | $47 | $56,389 |
| LHD 1 Amphibious Assault | $69 | $1,427 | $9,986 | N/A | $10,055 |

[a]Production Arsenal Ships were assumed to have a $450 million USP, with an added 20 percent procurement factor covering costs not included in the USP. The construction of the demonstrator, plus its operational demonstration expense, was assumed to cost $440 million (Phase III and IV funding). Its conversion is assumed to cost $200 million. Government costs during Phase V are assumed to be $30 million per year for eight years. Therefore, total costs are calculated as follows:

| | |
|---|---|
| $450M USP × 5 ships = | $2,250M |
| 20% Procurement Factor × $2,250M = | $450M |
| Demonstrator production = | $440M |
| Demonstrator conversion = | $200M |
| Government Management @ $30M/yr x 8 years = | $240M |
| Total (rounded up) = | $3,600M |

[b]Procurement includes contractor and government funding for Phases III, IV, and V. The figure is simply six times the $600 million average unit procurement cost.

[c]Five of the 19 ships are conversions, and 14 are new builds.

To be consistent with the other systems, we include Phase I and II funding for the Arsenal Ship program in Table C.2's Development Funding column. Funding estimates for Phases III–V are included in procurement, providing consistency with lead-ship funding in the procurement accounts for the other programs. Arsenal Ship system development and integration activities were expected to take place in Phase III; we therefore include most of its development costs under the Production Funding column.

The Arsenal Ship's development funding as shown in Table C.2 is consistent with the compared systems, with the exception of the DDG 51. The AEGIS combat system took the majority of the development funding in that program. In the 12 years since the DDG 51 contract was awarded, the development cost estimate for the Aegis combat system has more than doubled, from an original estimate of $1.4 billion to the current estimate of $2.9 billion. It seems clear that none understood its development cost at the time of the DDG-51 contract award.

### Procurement Costs

Unit procurement costs in Table C.2 for the three auxiliary ship programs range between $240 million and $684 million; the range for the three combatants is from $772 million to more than $1.4 billion. The Arsenal Ship unit procurement cost of $600 million is consistent with, yet was developed completely independently from, program costs as estimated by the Congressional Research Service.[8] We believe the $600 million number is optimistic.

In our comparison of the Arsenal Ship and combatant programs using the above data, we must consider projected versus actual cost estimates and total production quantity. Actual costs produce more accurate data than do projections. Larger production quantities result in lower unit costs, and when contracting with more than one

---

[8]*Navy/DARPA Arsenal Ship Program: Issues and Options for Congress* CRS Report for Congress, 97-455 F, April 1997, pp. 27–28. CRS estimates the initial cost of a depopulated demonstrator at $440 million (funding of Phases III & IV), its conversion at $200 million, and the unit procurement costs (including government costs) of the five follow-on ships at $472.5–605 million. Using the same calculation methodology as the estimates in Table C.2 would result in an average unit procurement cost range of $500–610 million for the six ships.

shipyard, the resulting competition is believed to reduce unit costs as well.

The lead-ship production contract for the LPD 17 program was awarded in December 1996. Its unit procurement cost estimates, like those of the Arsenal Ship program, reasonably represent expected expenditures. Twelve LPD 17 ships are planned, twice the number of the Arsenal Ship program.

Unit procurement costs in the DDG 51 program are well understood, as about half the 57 ships have been built or are currently under construction. The program's estimated per-unit production cost, adjusted for quantity changes, has increased 5 percent.[9] The quantity of vessels in this program is almost an order of magnitude larger than was planned for the Arsenal Ship. The DDG-51 program has also benefited from competition between multiple shipyards building the vessels.[10]

The LHD 1 program is almost complete; thus, its production cost estimates virtually represent actual expenditures. In the 13 years since the lead-ship contract was awarded, the program's estimated per-unit production cost has declined 13 percent.[11] The program's seven planned ships number one more than that of the Arsenal Ship program.

The cost histories from the two combatant programs begun in the 1980s suggest that the ship procurement cost estimates made at the time of the lead-ship contract award were fairly accurate. However, in both programs, the planned number of ships has more than doubled since the lead vessel contract was awarded.[12] The increases in quantity may have held down unit costs in both programs.

---

[9]Taken from RAND's Defense System Cost Performance Database, updated through December 1996 but not yet published.

[10]Because of the quantity of ships each yard will build, each should realize economies of scale.

[11]Taken from RAND's Defense System Cost Performance Database, updated through December 1996 but not yet published.

[12]The LHD 1 ship quantity increased from three to seven, and the DDG-51 ship quantity increased from 14 to 57.

The ASJPO indicated throughout the program's duration, and the contractor teams agreed, that excessive cost growth in the Arsenal Ship program would trigger its cancellation. We do not predict whether these sentiments would have persisted. Had the program continued, the demonstrator cost almost certainly would have exceeded the planned Phase III funds; the additional funding needed to construct a demonstrator representative of the production configuration is unknown. Doubling Phase III funding would have added $440 million to the program. Spreading this over the fleet of six ships would have increased the individual ship budgets by more than $70 million.

If the Navy had elected to continue the program, and funded Phase III as needed, subsequent Arsenal Ships might very well have met the $450 million USP requirement. We are confident in this estimate because the ASJPO and the contractors thought it achievable under the assumption that all development work was completed in Phase III. In addition, the history of relatively stable costs in the LHD and DDG programs indicates that the Navy and contractors understand recurring production costs, even early in these types of programs.

At one of our end of Phase I interviews, which was with one of the contractor teams that survived into Phase II, the contractor stated that its initial USP estimate for the Arsenal Ship using the traditional Navy acquisition approach was $895 million. Additional procurement items, government costs, and nonrecurring costs would increase this figure to well over $1 billion for average unit procurement. This appears to be a credible estimate for executing the program using the contemporary acquisition approach. When comparing the technical characteristics and complexity of the Arsenal Ship concept to the three combatants and their costs as shown above, a projected average unit procurement cost of $600–700 million for the Arsenal Ship fleet represents a substantial saving.

# ARSENAL SHIP CAPABILITIES DOCUMENT[1]

This ship capabilities document (SCD) complements the Arsenal Ship Concept of Operations (CONOPS) and provides definition of technical attributes that have evolved as part of ongoing study efforts. This SCD describes functions and capabilities for the Arsenal ships that should be treated as goals when conducting trade studies against the cost thresholds.

## 1.0 Design Philosophy

**1.1 Arsenal Ship.** The Arsenal Ships are to be delivered fully equipped for fleet operations. They are to have maximized system performance consistent with the CONOPS and the SCD within the cost constraint. The Arsenal Ships should achieve commonality with current Navy systems whenever possible. Innovative approaches that leverage existing DoD investments are strongly encouraged.

**1.2 Arsenal Ship Demonstrator.** The Arsenal Ship Demonstrator may not initially have the full capability of the Arsenal Ships. The demonstration program must show that the Arsenal Ships are suitable for performing their mission within the price thresholds. To this end, its objectives are to demonstrate:

1. The performance of the mission for 90 days.

2. The required architecture, communications, and essential data link functions to support the Arsenal Ship CONOPS.

---

[1]Taken from the Arsenal Ship Concept of Operations, Attachment 2 to Arsenal Ship Program Solicitation, 23 May 1996.

3. The capability for remote launch of strike, area Anti-Air Warfare (AAW) and fire support weapons. It is envisioned that the test program will include:

    a. Salvo launch of up to three Tomahawk missiles in three minutes

    b. Single SM2 launch using the Arsenal Ship as a remote magazine for a CEC (Cooperative Engagement Capability) ship

    c. Single Tomahawk launch using the Arsenal Ship as a remote magazine for air directed and shore based targeting

    d. Single weapon launch from a VLS Cell in support of a naval surface fire control mission digital call for fire.

4. That passive survivability will be sufficient for the expected operating scenarios.

The Arsenal Ship Demonstrator is to be capable of being converted to full mission ship capabilities and configuration and used as a fleet asset.

## 2.0   Warfighting Capabilities

**2.1   General.** The Arsenal Ship should be capable of firing a variety of weapons in support of a land campaign, including Long Range Strike, Invasion Stopping, Fire Support to Joint Ground Forces, Tactical Ballistic Missile Defense and Air Superiority.

**2.2   Launching System.** The ship should have about 500 VLS (vertical launch system) cells capable of launching current and planned vertical launch weapons. The actual number of VLS cells is to be recommended by optimizing the survivability, performance, sustainability and cost.

The ship is to have space, weight and support system capacity reservations for future installation of an extended range gun system.

**2.3   Connectivity.** Targeting, mission planning and command/decision functions will be offboard. The Arsenal Ship is to be connected to command platforms using the CEC "remote magazine" concept or an equivalent data link. An OTH satellite link capability is also to be provided. The ship is to be capable of full time communications with other ships, aircraft, satellites, and shore stations by means of responsive, reliable, clear and secure voice, tactical information distribution and recorded communications. Redundant links may be necessary to achieve robust interconnectivity. It is important that the Arsenal Ship be able to connect to existing joint force communications with minimum impact.

**2.4 Survivability.** The Arsenal Ship is required to be highly survivable in the entire littoral environment. Furthermore, consistent with the objectives for the Arsenal Ship to be an inexpensive platform with low life cycle costs, its survivability should be achieved through passive means to the extent practicable. Passive techniques to be considered include the use of signature control and countermeasures to make it difficult to detect, target and hit the ship, design/systems that will protect the VLS from damage if the ship is hit, and considerations of ship designs such that the ship will be virtually "unsinkable."

It is expected that the offeror will perform analyses to consider a range of current and future threat systems in performing trade-off studies to develop appropriate levels of survivability that can be achieved within the USP. The threats should include sub-surface, surface and airborne systems. These analyses/trades shall lead to determinations if and where limited active self defense systems are needed to augment the passive design considerations, consistent with minimizing crew size and cost constraints.

The ship shall be able to operate in a chemical-biological-radiation (CBR) environment.

Ship features shall be provided to contribute to the ship's ability to stay afloat and resist further damage including: fire fighting systems, inherent ship stability in damaged conditions, redundant electrical and other support systems.

**2.5 Mobility.** The ship is to be capable of a sustained speed (80% of installed power) of at least 22 knots. The ship is to carry sufficient fuel to conduct a 90 day mission. The ship shall be capable of continuous, precise navigation under all conditions, day or night, independent of geographic location, weather and visibility.

**2.6   Stowage Space.** The ship shall be capable of storing of consumables and repair parts for a 90 day mission consistent with the maintenance concept.

**3.0   Design Standards.** The design life of the ship is to be 35 years.

**3.1   Life Cycle Considerations.** The ships are to be manned, if at all, by a Navy crew to be as small as practicable, but in any event not to exceed 50 people.

The ship shall be ready to perform its missile launch mission when called upon. Availability is the measure of readiness selected for the ship systems. The ship shall be designed, constructed, and integrated with a total ship inherent availability goal of 0.95.

Equipment and material selection, equipment arrangement, built-in-test equipment, redundancy, equipment reliability, manning, logistics facilities, transportation, replenishment, on-board storage, training, and use of off-board support teams and spares pools are to be developed so as to minimize life cycle cost. The maintenance concept shall be developed to achieve the availability goals but a minimal life cycle cost. The maintenance concept shall be consistent with the Forward Operating Base Concept of the CONOPS.

Material selection, equipment arrangement, built-in-test equipment, redundancy, equipment reliability, manning, logistics facilities, transportation, replenishment, on-board storage, training, and use of off-board support teams and spares pools are to be developed so as to minimize operating and support (O&S) costs and be consistent with the CONOPS.

**3.2   Buoyancy and Stability.** The Ship is to have sufficient reserve buoyancy and stability to withstand flooding as a result of underwater damage. The ship is to withstand grounding or weapons damage that causes a leakage length of 15% of the hull waterline length, assuming the worst combination of flooded and non-flooded compartments within the overall damaged length. The undamaged ship is to have adequate stability to withstand the effects of 100 knot winds and accompanying seas. Stability is to be satisfactory both in full load departure and light load returning condition.

### 3.3 Design and Building Margins and Service Life Reserves.

Design and Building Margins are the responsibility of the offeror.

Service Life Reserves are ship and system capacities in the ship as completed that allow the ship to accept normal growth, planned and unplanned, during fleet service. The following margins are goals for service life of the ship after fleet acceptance of the Arsenal Ships:

- 20% electric power reserves

- 20% air conditioning capacity reserves

- 10% full load displacement growth

- 1 ft of full load center of gravity rise

The Service Life Reserves are exclusive of any margins for items specifically identified as space and weight capabilities.

**3.4 Regulatory Capabilities.** The ship design is to comply with 1972 COLREGS for-International-Inland and shall satisfy all the capabilities necessary to obtain certification for transit of the Suez Canal and Panama Canal. Rules-of-the-road equipment may be retracted or covered during low signature military operations.

**3.5 Standardization.** Standardization philosophy is to maximize system performance at the lowest life cycle cost while achieving commonality with current Navy systems wherever possible.

**3.6 Fuel.** The propulsion plant and ship service auxiliaries are to be designed to use Diesel Fuel Marine (DFM), corresponding to NATO Code F-76.

**3.7 Electric Plant Subsystem.** The ship service generating units are to be of a rating and number such that with one unit inoperable, the remaining installed capacity is able to carry the worst case electric load. At least two sources of electric power are to be provided to all mission critical components.

**3.8 Underway Replenishment.** The ship is to be able to be refueled while underway from standard Navy auxiliary ships. Vertical replenishment of provisions is required. Re-arming of VLS cells at sea is not required.

**3.9   Aviation Support.** The ship is to be provided with helicopter facilities that meet day and night operations, Visual Meteorological Conditions, landing area with limited service facilities certification for SH-60, V-22 and CH-46 aircraft.

**3.10   Environment.** The ship is to be capable of operating between latitudes of 70° North and 60° South. The ships shall not be operated in pack ice. All equipment and machinery installed in exposed locations are to retain full system capability in –40° F to 120° F air temperatures with simultaneous winds up to 40 knots true. All ship systems are to retain full system capability in 28° F to 95° F sea temperatures. All ship systems are to retain full capability with external relative humidity of 0% to 100%.

**3.11   Machinery Rating Temperatures.** Rated propulsion power and electric capacity shall be available with 100° F air temperature at prime mover inlet(s).

**3.12   Performance in a Seaway.** The ship is to meet the following capabilities:

1. Sea state 5:  replenish and strikedown underway

2. Sea state 6:  continuous efficient operation (other than replenishment)

3. Sea state 7:  limited operation, and capability of continuing its mission without returning to port for repairs after the sea subsides

4. Sea state 8 and above:  survivability without serious damage to mission-essential systems.

All structure and fittings are to be designed to withstand dynamic forces produced by motion of a ship in a seaway without operation of any ship stabilization system.

**3.13   Environmental Loading.** Environmental loading for ship, ship structure, and exposed equipment for design purposes are as follows:

1. Wind loading on vertical projected area, 30lb./sq. ft.

2. Snow and ice loading on horizontal projected area, 7.5lb./sq. ft.

3. Wave slap load on equipment expected to be exposed to green water, 500lb./sq. ft.

**3.14   Pollution Control.** The ship is to meet all applicable Federal and International environmental regulations.

**3.15   Personnel and Equipment Safety.** The ship is to be designed and constructed to meet internal airborne noise capabilities appropriate to a compartment's function. All installed equipment shall maintain operational effectiveness when exposed to electromagnetic fields as follows: 200v/m for topside mounted equipment, 10v/m for below decks equipment, and 3 Oersteds from below deck equipment. The installed equipment shall satisfy the capabilities for the prevention of Hazards of Electromagnetic Radiation to Personnel (HERP) and Ordnance (HERO).

# ARSENAL SHIP CONCEPT OF OPERATIONS[1]

The arsenal ship concept is a direct outgrowth of the Navy's shift in focus from the open ocean to the littoral. It is fully consistent with "Forward . . . from the Sea", and "Operational Maneuver from the Sea", and addresses current as well as anticipated future requirements for more decisive, responsive and varied naval support to the land battle. Through concentration of massive firepower, continuous availability and application of netted targeting and weapons assignment, the arsenal ship will increase dramatically the scope and relevance of surface strike and fire support. Tailored specifically to meet the heavy support challenge in the opening days of conflict, arsenal ship will bring firepower to bear in support of Unified CinC's and ground commander plans and schemes of maneuver as well as provide significant leverage during the early phases of crises response and control.

## OVERVIEW

As the foremost world power, the United States will continue to maintain global interests, and therefore must be able to influence and respond to events with credible military presence and power projection capabilities. In the face of steadily decreasing overseas basing and a shrinking military budget, the United States must maintain the ability, in concert with allies, to execute timely combat operations across the spectrum of conflict. Naval forces, sustaining for-

---

[1]Taken from Arsenal Ship Concept of Operations, Attachment 1 to Arsenal Ship Program Solicitation, 23 May 1996.

ward presence, will be key to successful introduction as well as early employment of ground forces.

Arsenal ship represents an affordable and much needed enhancement to our existing force of carriers and land attack capable combatants and submarines. It is not a replacement for these or for land-base air. Instead, it is part of the whole—just as the Battleship was a part of the whole for nearly a century. Operating under the control and umbrella of regularly deployed Aegis combatants, arsenal ship will supply substantial firepower early, giving unified Commanders-in-Chief (CinCs) the capability to halt or deter invasion and, if necessary, enable the build-up of coalition land-based air and ground forces to achieve favorable conflict resolution. With a force totaling about six, arsenal ships will be stationed continuously forward, always available for rapid movement upon receipt of even ambiguous or limited strategic warning. Much like our maritime pre-positioning force, they will remain on station in support of a Unified CinC for indefinite periods without dependence on host nation support or permission.

## OPERATIONAL CONCEPT

With about 500 missiles and space for future extended range gun systems, arsenal ships will be capable of launching many current and planned Department of Defense weapons across the warfare spectrum. Arsenal ship can be positioned to destroy the enemy's critical infrastructure at or near the inception of hostilities. Using precision guided missiles equipped with advanced penetrating warheads and sub munitions, this ship will serve as an additional maneuver element in the landing force or ground force commander's plan by isolating, immobilizing, or destroying enemy forces, including enemy armored fighting vehicles, as well as providing fires in direct tactical support of ground forces.

Employing the Cooperative Engagement Capability (CEC) "remote magazine" launch concept, the Arsenal Ship will provide additional magazine capacity for Theater Ballistic Missile Defense (TBMD) and Air Supremacy missiles. This concept allows for remote missile selection, on-board missile initialization and remote launch orders, and provides remote "missile away" messages to the control platform.

To meet mission goals at affordable cost, ship design will be based on commercial practices and rely extensively on automation in engineering, damage, ship and weapon control systems to achieve a crew size of no more than 50. Berthing spaces for special evolution detachments will enhance operational flexibility.

Arsenal ship and associated weapon control systems will have the flexibility to be responsive to multiple commanders and to conduct simultaneous Long Range Strike, Naval Surface Fire Support, and Theater Air Defense missions. Tables E.1 and E.2 are representative of the type of capabilities desired.

## OPERATING ASSUMPTIONS

Arsenal Ship is a firepower multiplier that, in conjunction with other naval forces, increases decisively the options available to the theater CinC. The operational concept for Arsenal Ships is based on the following assumptions.

Table E.1

Target Sets to be Countered by Arsenal Ship

|  | Halt Invasion | Long Range Strike | Battlespace Dominance | Surface Fire Support |
|---|---|---|---|---|
| Complex Adaptive Armed Forces | Air Land Maneuver Battle Groups (e.g., OMGs) | National / Regional C4I Space Control | Manned A/C TBMs, UAVs Cruise Missiles SAM/AAA | Long-Range Artillery TBMs Logistics Assets |
| Armored Mech Armed Forces | Armor-Heavy Comb. Arms Formations Divisions/BDEs | National and Regional C4I | Manned A/C TBMs SAM/AAA | Long-Range Artillery |
| Infantry Based Armed Forces | Armor/Mech "Pure" units (BDEs/BNs) | Military Region District C4I | Manned A/C SAM/AAA | Medium-Range Artillery Logistics Assets |
| Internal Security Light Force | Transportation Railroads Trucking, Light Vehicles | National CMD Authority Military Concentrations | OP Bases Light A/C Coastal Patrol Craft | Logistics Assets Economic Asset Local Forces |

**Table E.2**

**Weapons to Counter Target Sets**

| | Halt Invasion | Long Range Strike | Battlespace Dominance | Surface Fire Support |
|---|---|---|---|---|
| Complex Adaptive Armed Forces | SM-2/ATACMS-BAT SLAM TLAM-BAT TLAM-C | TLAM | ATACMS TLAM-C/D SM-2 Blk III A/B and Blk IVA SM-2 LEAP | ATACMS, SLAM, STRIKE-SM TLAM-C/D NAVAL GUNFIRE (VGAS/SCRAM) |
| Armored Mechanized Armed Forces | SM-2/ATACMS-BAT TLAM-BAT SLAM STRIKE-SM | SM2/ATACMS-BAT TLAM-BAT SLAM STRIKE-SM | ATACMS TLAM-C/D SM-2 Blk III A/B and Blk IVA | ATACMS, SLAM, STRIKE-SM TLAM-C/D NAVAL GUNFIRE (VGAS/SCRAM) |
| Infantry Based Armed Forces | ATACMS SLAM STRIKE-SM | TLAM-D ATACMS-ER | ATACMS | ATACMS, SLAM STRIKE-SM TLAM-C/D NAVAL GUNFIRE (VGAS/SCRAM) |
| Internal Security Light Force | NAVAL GUNFIRE (VGAS/SCRAM) | TLAM-C | ATACMS NAVAL GUNFIRE (VGAS/SCRAM) | ATACMS NAVAL GUNFIRE (VGAS/SCRAM) |

**CinC Requirements.** Arsenal Ships will be assigned to theater CinC to provide:

- *Conventional Deterrence* against regional aggression inimical to U.S. interests,

- *Flexible response* for demonstration of power independent of diplomatic limitations,

- *Credible forward firepower* support to joint and coalition land forces early in a regional contingency if deterrence fails. The forward theater arsenal ship weapon loadout will be robust, flexible and tailorable to CinC requirements in order to expand CinC options for use of assigned joint forces.

**Joint Warfighting.** Arsenal ships will be fully integrated into the joint warfighting force structure. The ships will be capable of firing a variety of weapons in support of a land campaign, including Long Range Strike, Invasion Stopping, Fire Support to Joint Ground Forces, Tactical Ballistic Missile Defense and Air Superiority.

**Forward Operations.** Arsenal Ships will be stationed, operated and supported in forward theaters for conventional deterrence and to provide immediate responsiveness  upon onset of hostilities.  The three forward theaters currently envisioned for arsenal ships are:

- Central Command (Southwest Asia / Persian Gulf)

- Pacific Command (Western Pacific)

- European Command (Mediterranean).

## COMMAND AND CONTROL

Arsenal ships will operate in both peace and war as integral fleet units within the chain of command under Joint Combatant Command (COCOM). Peacetime Operational Control (OPCON) will normally be exercised by numbered fleet commanders.  Within a Joint Task Force structure, OPCON will normally be exercised by the Joint Force Maritime Commander.  Tactical Command (TACON) will normally be assigned to a naval commander.

## JOINT CONNECTIVITY MISSION PLANNING AND TARGETING

Key to both arsenal ship's affordability and operational flexibility is off-board integration of all but the most rudimentary C4I. Joint connectivity, including targeting, mission planning, and weapons control will be provided to arsenal ship through the existing fleet of Aegis cruisers and destroyers.  Employing an advanced, CEC-like weapons link, the wide array of joint connectivity needed for netted operations will be hosted through an assigned control ship.  The role of target and user integration will similarly be performed off-ship, thereby significantly reducing arsenal ship manning, cost and developmental risk; while leveraging the extensive joint $C^4I$ investment (Link 16, CEC, etc.) already programmed for the majority of the Surface Navy.

The complexity of varied tasking will be reduced to highly reliable, jam resistant targeting, weapons, and launch orders.

## SURVIVABILITY

Though arsenal ship will operate in any threat environment under the protective umbrella of battle force combatants, it must be survivable against 21st century anti-ship missiles, torpedoes, and mines. Passive defense should capitalize on the benefits of mass (tonnage), innovative applications of multiple hull integrity, and signature reduction. Active self defense if required should be roughly equivalent to that of a combat logistics force ship.

## MAINTENANCE

Arsenal ships are to be forward deployed for the large part of their operational lives. Low maintenance and high reliability must be engineered into ship design to assure high operational availability.

# JOINT MEMORANDUM—ARSENAL SHIP PROGRAM

Assistant Secretary of the Navy
(Research Development and Acquisition)
Washington, D.C. 20350-1000
Director, Defense Advanced Research Project Agency
Arlington, VA 22203-1714
March 18, 1996

JOINT MEMORANDUM

MEMORANDUM FOR COMMANDER, NAVAL SEA SYSTEMS
COMMAND
CHIEF OF NAVAL RESEARCH

Subj: ARSENAL SHIP PROGRAM

This joint memorandum establishes the Arsenal Ship Program, and provides the Director, Defense Advanced Research Project Agency (DARPA), Commander, Naval Sea Systems Command (NAVSEA) and Chief of Naval Research (CNR) with precepts regarding the basic requirements, goals, and acquisition strategy for the program.

The basic requirement for the Arsenal Ship is to satisfy joint naval expeditionary force warfighting requirements in regional conflicts by providing the theater commander with massive firepower, long range strike, and flexible targeting and possible theater defense through the availability of hundreds of VLS cells. To meet this warfare requirement affordably, the Arsenal Ship concept and design must be straightforward and simple. Detailed requirements and concept of operations are defined in separate documentation, however, key elements for the Arsenal Ship include:

- Provide approximately 500 VLS cells, with the capability to launch Navy and joint weapons to support the land campaign;

- Integrate the combat system with Cooperative Engagement Capability (CEC) links to serve in, or as, the off-board control;

- Appropriate ship design features for survivability and ship self defense which could be incorporated at a later date if needed;

- Low ownership costs through the use of innovative maintenance and operational methods, procedures, and technologies;

- Crew size will not exceed 50 personnel. The design objective will be to minimize crew size to the maximum extent below 50 which is technically feasible.

In the face of limited budget levels, the use of acquisition reform initiatives and streamlined contracting methods are paramount to meet the basic requirements of the Arsenal Ship in an affordable manner. To accomplish this, a non-acquisition category demonstrator ship shall be developed that will be convertible to a fleet asset at a future date.

In addition, cost must be viewed as an independent variable, and early industry involvement with the development of a cooperative industry-government team are viewed as key to achieving our goals. To minimize cost, off-the shelf systems will be used exclusively. Any development of new systems will require the approval of ASN (RD&A). The cost of acquiring the first ship will not exceed $520 million including the cost of concept development and competition. These funds will be provided jointly by the Navy and DARPA with contributions of $350 million and $170 million respectively. For FY 96, funds will be provided by re-programming. For FY 97, funds will be requested as part of the budget request. The Program Objectives Memorandum process will be used to provide the remaining funding.

The Director, DARPA; Commander, NAVSEA; and CNR are tasked to establish a plan for a joint Arsenal Ship Advanced Technology

Demonstrator Program Office and identify to the ASN (RD&A) a candidate full-time program manager. The program manager will work closely with OPNAV staffs to ensure that requirements are understood and fully met, and with industry in a team approach to ship development and construction. The Arsenal Ship Program Office (ASPO) should operate as a "skunk works" organization, eliminating or streamlining acquisition procedures, processes, and paperwork. The ASPO shall be comprised of representatives from DARPA, NAVSEA and CNR with a total maximum number of 9 personnel. DARPA will initially have program lead with transition to NAVSEA at an appropriate time during ship production. This program represents a good opportunity to take advantage of DARPA's culture and experience in prototyping to transition alternative business practices into how the Navy buys ships. The ASPO shall be initially located in the National Capitol Region and later co-located at the shipyard chosen to construct the first ship.

DARPA, NAVSEA, and CNR are directed to develop a detailed plan of action, milestones, technology initiatives, acquisition strategy, and budget necessary to execute the Arsenal Ship Program, with the goal to have a demonstrator Arsenal Ship at sea by the year 2000. Specific recommendations and actions necessary to accelerate ship development should be the focus of the plan, eliminating all procedures that are not specifically required by law. The plan should also provide systems integration approach and affordability initiatives to reduce acquisition and ownership costs.

The Arsenal Ship Program is among the highest programs within the Navy. All organizations and contractors participating in and supporting the Arsenal Ship Program should view it with priority, and proceed with a sense of urgency to achieve the goal of beginning demonstrator ship at-sea testing of the Navy's first Arsenal Ship in the year 2000.

# MEMORANDUM OF AGREEMENT—JOINT NAVY/ DARPA PROGRAM

### MEMORANDUM OF AGREEMENT (MOA) JOINT NAVY/DARPA ARSENAL SHIP DEMONSTRATION PROGRAM

**Purpose:**

The purpose of this document is to establish a joint Navy/DARPA agreement as to the objectives, roles and responsibilities, schedule, and funding for the Arsenal Ship demonstration program.

**Background:**

Arsenal Ship is a high priority program for the Navy to acquire a new capability for delivery of large quantities of ordnance in support of land and littoral engagements. Key to both Arsenal Ship's afford-ability and operational flexibility is off-board integration of all but the most rudimentary C4I. The ships are conceived to be theater as-sets that will operate under the authority of the joint Commanders-In-Chief (CINCs) and will receive their targeting along with com-mand and decision information from other assets. Early in Arsenal Ship's life this control will be exercised through an Aegis platform, though as other assets mature, control will transition to aircraft such as AWACS or an E-2 with CEC-like capability and eventually to the Marine or Army shooter on the ground. Thus, the Arsenal Ship will not be fitted with long range surveillance or fire control sensors, but will be remotely controlled via robust data links. The data links will be secure, redundant and anti-jam in order to provide high reliability in the connectivity of the Arsenal Ships in high jamming operational scenarios. The program overall is an attempt to leverage the significant current joint investment in Link 16 and CDC. The Arsenal Ship's survivability will be primarily achieved through passive design techniques. While active systems are not ruled out, they must be consistent with overall cost and manning goals. These design goals will allow the Arsenal Ship to have a very small crew (potentially, none at all) which will be a key ingredient in minimizing its life cycle costs. It is expected that the Arsenal Ship will transit and operate independently but when in a hostile environment, its defense will be enhanced by working cooperatively with other elements of the force. It is envisioned that the Arsenal Ship will be a large hull designed so that the weapons carried onboard are protected from damage and the ship is "virtually unsinkable" if hit by missiles, torpedoes, or mines.

This demonstration program is a non-ACAT program that has been created to evaluate this new capability while minimizing the risks in acquisition of approximately six ships (to include conversion of the Arsenal Ship Demonstrator to a fleet operational unit at low cost). To ensure that the program remains affordable, a firm cost threshold for the production ships has been established. This program will be conducted using DARPA's Section 845 Agreements Authority so as to allow industry wide latitude in satisfying the Navy's requirements within this threshold. Agreements will be structured to allow trade-offs between cost and performance. Program success will be judged by the extent to which the Arsenal Ship meets operational requirements.

A second purpose for this demonstration program is to accelerate the Navy's ongoing acquisition reform activities focused on buying improved ships at a lower cost. To this end, the joint program will focus on exploiting DARPA's culture and experience in prototyping system programs. We anticipate the production Arsenal Ship contracts will serve as a model for future streamlining.

**Technical Objectives:**

The Arsenal Ship is intended to provide a large quantity of (approximately 500) vertical launch systems (VLS) with the capability to launch a variety of weapons for strike, fire support, and area air defense. The exact number of VLS missiles will be determined during the program by optimizing the survivability, performance, sustainability and costs.  The demonstration program will highlight Arsenal Ship's capability as a force multiplier to the Marine Corps, Army, and full array of joint forces.  In that regard, it is recognized that certain weapons do not yet exist in the inventory that would allow the full capability to be demonstrated for all missions.  No new weapons developments or significant enhancements to weapons are to be pursued as part of this program.  Instead, demonstrations should be planned and structured such that significant communications, architecture, and data link functions are evaluated.  The goal of the program will be to achieve a balanced design that satisfies the thresholds consistent with the ship's concept of operations (CONOPS).

The demonstration program must show that the production Arsenal Ships are suitable for performing their mission within prescribed cost constraints.  To this end, its objectives are to demonstrate:

1. The performance of the mission for 90 days.

2. The architecture, communications, and data link functions to satisfy the Arsenal Ship CONOPS.

3. The capability for remote launch of strike, area air warfare and fire support weapons.  It is envisioned that the test program will include:

    a)  Salvo launch of up to 3 Tomahawk missiles in 3 minutes.

    b)  Single SM2 launch using the arsenal ship as a remote magazine for a Cooperative Engagement Capability (CEC) ship

    c)  Single Tomahawk launch using the arsenal ship as a remote magazine for air directed and shore based targeting

    d)  Single weapon launch from a VLS cell in support of a naval surface fire control mission digital call for fire

4. That the proper balance between passive survivability and active self defense will be sufficient for the expected operating scenarios.

**Cost Threshold: Industry Goal—$450M/Program Threshold— $550M**

The acquisition cost threshold is based on the average Navy SCN end costs for the five follow ships acquired after this demonstration program, expressed in FY98 dollars. The costs of the weapons are not included.

**Life Cycle Costs:**

Industry will be tasked to perform the life cycle cost analyses to demonstrate the operating and support costs for their Arsenal Ship design over a 20 year life. This will ensure that the tenets of the program including reduced manning and innovative operating concepts remain focused on minimizing life cycle costs.

**Schedule:**

The goal of the demonstration program is to have the ship in the water and ready to start meaningful testing in the year 2000. The program manager will maintain a detailed schedule toward this end and present the plan for approval by the Steering Committee. The basic acquisition strategy for this program is to maximize industry involvement through a competitive multi-phase approach to encourage the maximum innovation within the limits of the cost thresholds. The Government, through the program office, will coordinate with industry to ensure the availability of information that the industry teams need to make informed trades.

**Funding:**

The cost of the R&D program for this demonstration Arsenal Ship will not exceed $520 million including the cost of concept development and competition. These funds will be provided jointly by the Navy and DARPA as follows:

| | | | (Dollars in millions) | | | | |
| --- | --- | --- | --- | --- | --- | --- | --- |
| | FY96 | FY97 | FY98 | FY99 | FY00 | FY01 | Total |
| Navy | $4.0 | $25.0 | $141.0 | $90.0 | $80.0 | $10.0 | $350.0 |
| DARPA | $1.0 | $15.0 | $47.0 | $50.0 | $36.0 | $21.0 | $170.0 |

The Navy will provide its share of the funds to DARPA at the beginning of each fiscal year.

**Roles and Responsibilities:**

This joint Navy/DARPA demonstration program will be conducted under the auspices of DARPA's Section 845 Agreements Authority. DARPA will lead the demonstration program and will transition the leadership to the Navy in the later stages of the program, upon mutual agreement of the parties.

The program will be managed by a joint Navy/DARPA program office with the Program Manager reporting to DARPA. A small program office is envisioned. DARPA, Naval Sea Systems Command (NAVSEA), and the Office of Naval Research (ONR) will initially each provide two billets. It is expected that the program office will grow to a maximum of three billets each as the program grows to maturity.

The Navy shall develop a concept of operations (CONOPS) for the program that will be reviewed and considered for update as the program develops. The program office will use the CONOPS to guide the trade studies to be conducted by industry.

The Program Manager will develop a program plan including major decision milestones, and the development of a program transition plan. The Steering Committee will approve the initial program plan and thereafter will conduct quarterly reviews to assess progress and provide guidance to the Program Manager.

The Steering Committee will be as follows:

Director, TTO—DARPA Chairman

Deputy Assistant Secretary of the Navy (DASN, Ships)

Assistant Director, TTO for Maritime Programs—DARPA

Director, Surface Warfare Plans/Programs/Requirements Branch—OPNAV (N863)

PEO for Surface Combatants

Office of Naval Research (ONR33)

An Executive Committee consisting of:

> Assistant Secretary of the Navy (RD&A)
> Director of Surface Warfare (N86)
> Director, DARPA
> Commander, NAVSEA
> Chief of Naval Research

will review the program at major decision milestones to evaluate the validity of program cost thresholds and provide re-direction as necessary.

**Term of Agreement:**

It is expected that this MOA shall remain in effect for the duration of the demonstration program. Early termination of the program due to funding unavailability, lack of legal authority or other reason beyond the control of the parties shall be a basis for termination of this MOA. Any termination shall be preceded by consultation among the parties.